WalterMepham

Born March 14, 1898   Killed November 30, 1917,

Cambrai, France.

An auto-biographical Novel by M. Stow

Dedication

To the enduring memory of 7,048 officers and men of the forces of the British Empire who fell at the Battle of Cambrai, November 20–December 3, 1917, but have no known graves.

Chapters

Part One: Family

Chapter 1: Why We Went to War

Chapter 2: Father's Family

Chapter 3: Mother's Family

Chapter 4: Our Parents Meet

Part Two: For or Against

Chapter 5: Arthur Conan Doyle

Chapter 6: Lord Bertrand (Bertie) Russell

Chapter 7: Arthur Wells

Chapter 8: Alfred Byfield

Part Three: Sarajevo

Chapter 9: The Assassination in Sarajevo

Chapter 10: The Decision Is Made

Chapter 11: France

Chapter 12: Reports of War

Chapter 13: The Cambrai Operation

Chapter 14: At Flesquieres

Chapter 15: The Boulon Woods

Part Four: Louverval memorial, France, 14th March 1998 and November 30th 2017.

Author's Note

This is the story of Walter and his elder brother, Harry Arthur Mepham, of London, England, researched and compiled from the records of the time by his maternal distant cousin, the author, Malcolm Stow.

The idea for the story was prompted by a postcard found among the papers of the author's late grandmother, Henrietta Wells, with the starkly precise dates of birth and death of Walter, killed at the First World War Battle of Cambrai.

The story is embellished by selections from Sir Arthur Conan Doyle's field reports, *The British Campaign in France and Flanders* (unpublished); and Bertrand Russell's *The Ethics of War* (published

1915).

These two literary combatants were contemporaneously implicated in the life of Walter, and Harry Arthur. From the Mepham family history in Sussex, England, where Conan Doyle lived and supported encampment for soldiers travelling to the Western Front in 1915; and to Holborn, London, where the Mephams lived and worked in 1914, and where Russell also lived at the time. Russell argued against conscription, and for a personal rational existential choice, in war, or pacifism.

Both authors would have influenced Walter and Harry Arthur's decisions to go to war; and, in Harry's case, his refusal to return to the Somme battlefront, after 1917.

The family stories are fictionalized around such known facts; and the Mepham brother's likely discussions, and their own owned decisions, as to the outcome of those shared deliberations. What did it mean to fight a "good" war? For love of king and country, for purely personal pride? For bread on the table?

For their parents Caroline Wells, of East London, and Mark Henry Mepham from Kent and Suffolk, England; and for their own family cousins, and their children, and grandchildren yet to be born.

November 30th 1917.

Cambrai, France

Dear Harry Arthur,

I know how much it grieved you to hear of my being lost. How Mother was.

How she told you not to go back, and how all the emotion came down on you, and nearly killed you both. How, if Mother had lost us both, as well as Father, then her heart would have…Well, you know it wasn't you who killed her; it was me.

She knew. It was the dreaded question: Why did we all have to go, leaving her alone to tend wounded and dying soldiers—strangers—in our places?

When Father went to war, in 1915, well, that was one thing. Perhaps to persuade us, and her, that he would die for us, and in our stead. He might not see his grandchildren himself, but Mother would. And that we—one of us, at least—would have a better chance of bringing children, our parent's grandchildren, into the world and their being remembered in both Father's, and Mother's image.

I don't think they wanted both of us to go to the Great War.

War. As I am the younger brother, Father went in my stead. But then we brothers did both go, and there was no stopping us.

After you and Father went off full of gusto, not wishing but prepared to die. I was the insistent younger son wanting to follow in your footsteps. Prepared to die, to lie, too, about my age as Father did, younger not older lying, to join up.

And then father, you, and then myself, to be sent abroad. Overseas for the first time in our lives.

When I did eventually go, Mother must have felt deserted by all of us. But by me in particular. She knew there was no stopping me, and she kept her hurt to herself even when we were all together.

Do you remember, Harry? When you were on leave during the zeppelin air raids on Croydon in 1916?

It was then that I persuaded her to let me go, so that I could get back at those trying to kill us in our beds. By the time I was trained and set off later in 1916, the year you returned for leave, only for you to return again, to the second Battle of The Somme. That was the last time we saw each other, you know? Then, when news reached mother about my being lost at Cambrai, in 1917, you were home again. At the hospital, where mother was nursing the sick and injured and dying, perhaps, and she must have known I would not be coming back.

She persuaded you not to return. To abscond from leave, to desert, didn't she?

Did you try medical grounds, or simply refuse to return?

How could any of us be blamed? How could we feel disgust anymore, or hatred, or indifference now, or even some sympathy, perhaps. For those dressed up in self-serving political and religious conscientious objection, instead of the bloody uniform of war?

They, the Refusers, they refused for the same reasons, in the end, that we did go in the first place: each of us to save ourselves, and our family's future.

The same reason you absconded, Harry, and Mother persuaded you to so do; that you and yours, would be the next of our line, if mine were not.

For our family, Harry Arthur, you not only fought, but you found something in common with the no-conscription, white feather lot, the Peace Pledgers, didn't you? As well as with the fighting brigades, saving our country from invasion, you, and now me, Harry, saving *our own*…wretched-souls…*that* is what they call the foot-soldiers out here 'the poor bloody infantry' you know?

But most of all, for all of you. You, Harry Arthur, and mother found that my being missing, my uncertain death, although not glorious, would not be in vain. Father, believed his going in my stead, would not for any of us, to be in vain,

To my brother, from your loving brother,

Walter Mepham.

Aldershot Army Training Camp, Hampshire, England, 1916.

Part One: Family

Chapter 1: Why We Went to War

This is *our* story I write here, awaiting orders to be set off to France, or wherever. We do not yet know and are not told, and should I not return…

This is our story:

To Harry Arthur:

I, Walter, was born at home at 56 Walterton Road in the civil parish of Paddington, and registered by our parents at Marylebone in the county of Middlesex (west). We lived off Maida Hill among the plush mansions of Maida Vale and the Harrow Road, the new London suburbs, the grand streets and mews off Kensington by Warwick Road and the Great Western Road.

Over the Thames river at Putney, then the Trade Roads to Surrey; and then, on to Sussex and Kent where our father and his father, and our great grandfather, were born.

Our great-grandfather William Mepham was born in 1805.

An agricultural labourer, he began working from a young age, at less than 9 or 10 years, in the farmer's fields, while living at cottages on Nethersfield Green, Battle, near Hastings.

Where, in 1066, the Norman invasion of England was said to have taken place. A date we remember from school—you and me, Harry, we always liked our history, didn't we? On their way northward, over the South and North Downs—we always laughed at those peculiarly named places too: Going up the downs!—on their way those Normans took in Meopham, a Kentish town of the ancient land of Meapha. Meapha was ruled by an Anglo-Saxon Jute king from modern-day Germany.

Our German family name Mepham, must have been derived from the original village of that name. The earliest recording of the Mepham family name, so spelled, and in Kent, was in the sixteenth century. At Mepham, Kent, in the time of Henry the Eighth and Queen Elizabeth first.

Our Great-Grandfather William Mepham, was born in Kent, and later moved to Sussex, to have his family, by our Great-Mother Harriet and their only child, our grandfather Mark, surviving. And then, Mark, and Fanny, moving to Sussex; and then much later, our father Mark Henry Mepham, and mother Caroline Wells, after they moved to London, our grandparents in Hampshire, where you Harry Arthur, were born, in 1895; and then me. As far as the hilly north Thames shore. At Paddington, London where Mark met our mother Caroline Wells; and I, Walter, was later born, at home, Walterton Road, Maida Vale.

Our great-grandfather William, and Harriet, lived in Hampshire; originally, from Sussex, where William the Conqueror conquered all those years ago.

And I born and we living, at London where *that* William, of 1066, later crowned himself at St Paul's church as King William the First of the English. Now, 1916, there is another King William, threatening to invade. Kaiser Wilhelm of Germany, cousin to our own King George. Both cousins, genealogically of the Royal Tsar Alexander of Orthodox Russia and western Christianity. Now they, and all of us, are in this Great War together.

In 1914, the Russians, with Serbia, threatened the Austro-Hungarian and the German Kaiser Wilhelm threatened to invade England. As General Bismarck, it was said, would have endangered our shores, if the Germans had won the Prussian war, at Paris, back in 1871.

The war that anyway only then established The German Monarchy and Nationhood, from all those Protestant and Catholic Princedoms to which we in all of Great Britain are related.

As the French Revolution and Napoleonic Wars ended, in 1815, the French too may as well, may have invaded this "island of shopkeepers" as Napoleon was supposed to have called England.

When the then Prussian-German Frederich Wilhelm von Bulow, and Blucher, then came to our Duke of Wellington's Great British armies' rescue, at Waterloo, Belgium, near to Brussels, 1815.

Not *that* far from The Somme, Harry; where you too, are now fighting these battles again, Harry; and I expect soon to join you, soon.

The 'Frenchies' did not invade before, and the Bosch will not this time, either. We will see to that. We two brothers and our father, Mark Henry, set off to fight former allies and familial enemies - us and them - as all wars end up. Even all though we are all related in the end and we fight for our family; and for ours', and their royal families.

In 1815, great-grandfather William, at only ten years old, and would have been too young to fight that previous Great War in Europe.

Although someone told us here at Aldershot, why I could not tell, that in the Napoleonic Republic, and also the American Independence wars before. That in those wars, ten-year-old flag-bearers and drummer-boys were sent ahead in battle; and took the full blast of rifle and cannon fire.

I cannot imagine the reason for this, except the preservation of others - their elders, who could have more children, to replace them by. Or they were criminals, perhaps, cruelly treated. As you and I and the "poor bloody infantry" as Conan Doyle had us down – since the Boer Wars ended 1902 with apartheid, and peace - and as we will do again. There in France, and Belgium, and Germany, at once, and again. We will win, again.

On June 18th 1815, after the burning and retreat from Moscow in 1812, the final Battle of Waterloo was fought, and our great-grandfather William would have heard about *that* war spoken about in the houses, taverns, churches, and churchyards of Sussex. The battles, no doubt, would have been played out with toy soldiers, as we did as children in West London; before *this* war; and as we do now for real, and for our certain victory.

In those the same Flanders fields. As you described on your last leave, in Brighton with Mother and I there.

We had no word of Father, from Turkey, or from Africa where he was sent last. He was in the deserts of Africa - Egypt, we were told - or perhaps his workaday dream of going to Morocco, didn't we know, was eventually fulfilled? The land there in France is similar you told us, to that land of our great-grandfather's in Kent and Sussex: the village hamlets, wooded hills, and church spires.

And ourselves like those toy tin soldiers with row upon row of cavalry, foot soldiers, and cannon. We will again fight side-by-side, as we fought as children, brothers in arms. On the hillsides beyond figures emulating Napoleon and Wellington and Bismarck or Blucher, stand now again as the Generals, and newspaper report writers like Conan Doyle. Directing and reporting upon battle tactics and operations from afar.

Then, on the hills beyond, our enemy. Then. The troops, infantry and cavalry fusiliers, and artillery of the new nation of Republican France. Then, as now. Then, in 1815, the German Confederation. Bohemian, Bavarian, Saxon and Hanoverian, as our then our King George, the Fifth, of England. And we, as then, will be there in line, with the appointed Duke of Wellington, awaiting orders.

There, now that and both times around, the same line of copse and woods, fields and hilltop barns, and buildings, taken and re-taken. The rising taste of gunpowder to fill the air, and, in the rain, the sweat and blood of men and horses.

After the invasion and fall of Belgium, in August 1914, the threat of German invasion on France, and England, again to be realised.

We went to read the newspaper articles and visited the British Museum, in Holborn, London (west) where we then lived.

Often, Father took us to *The* Museum. We went to others, and to libraries, freely, and father told us all he knew - he knew a lot about it - and we liked our history. Especially that last bit about how this war, the Great War, got started.

For most who took notice of these events, war at first seemed impossible; then more and more likely, and then simply inevitable. Then, as if it just happened suddenly with that assassination of the Habsburg-Lorraine Archduke Franz Ferdinand, in Sarajevo, in 1914.

No time to consider our position, really.

France and Belgium were being invaded by the German armies for no apparent reason; except maybe, that they were finishing off unfinished business from 1871, maybe even the Russians for 1812. How we may trade unrelievedly on the past!

We had been warned by Arthur Conan Doyle about German trade and expansionism in Europe - as well as in the empires of France and these Great British Isles - in the newspapers we read, and then when you and Father left for foreign parts, this Great War was well underway.

What followed was the outbreak of this war— "The War to End All Wars". Which is really just another name for the disputes between the same Royal Families and their Colonial Trading Empires, in the lands of Africa, Asia and the Americas; in the Austro-Hungarian, Turkish Ottoman Empire, Palestine and Arabia, and Egypt, and as far as the Dutch and German Boer, in South Africa.

In Japan, China, India, Australia, and New Zealand. Countries that brought in the Greatest Empire the World has ever seen - The British Empire - and on which the sun would never set.

We didn't know what we were really fighting for until afterwards, and even then there would be big questions, with much left unclear. You see, as much as we thought we knew these things - the reasons why we went to war - these get all lost in the smoke screen, the fog of war. And then all that is left is ourselves, and our families, and my blessed - and my not then, but soon - now my

wretched soul, too, that I know.

Chapter 2: Father's Family

Great-grandfather William in Sussex, was a widower in 1831, when great-grandmother Harriet passed away, soon after giving birth to our grandfather Mark, their only child.

William and Mark, father and son, lived together by The Tide Mill, in the hamlet of Bishopstone Seaford, East Sussex. After William passed away in 1852, at the age of thirty-one, Mark married Fanny, a young woman from Sedgecombe, a nearby village.

They had their first child, Francis Lucy, in 1851, at Bishopstone. The family, leaving Kent, worked and stayed on at the tide mill, on the tidal inlet, known as East Beach Creek, Sussex.

Along the coastal Sheep Drove Road, the recently laid siding and station halt connected with the main railway line between Seaford and Newhaven, the then main Trade Ports on the English Channel and then as we by ship, across to Europe.

There was a flour mill holding a full sixteen pairs of grinding stones and large sluices to the seawater millpond, at the top of Tide Mills Village. Grandfather Mark worked there as a miller's labourer, and the family lived in a row of millers' cottages with other families, of field labourers, turners, grinders, sack men, and carters, most named after their trade as the Turners and Millers, as the Scotts were Scotts all working for mill-wright Thomas Parks, at the large Tide Mill House.

Our aunt Frances Lucy was born there, in their cottage, one year before our father, Mark Henry, was born. Named Mark, after his father, and Henry after Fanny's likely French family name; known in English as Harry. Father was only five years old when a terrible storm brought up flooding seawaters and shingle lifted from the beach. Filled the millponds, destroying many of the buildings at Tide Mills.

The family escaped, on horseback and trundling carts, all terrified in the rain and wind swept seawaters. They could all have been easily killed as some were, through crashing stones and bricks, father said.

Most of the houses became uninhabitable. The Tide Mills were eventually closed. The site was later used for artillery field practice by the Newhaven Fort, built in part from the rubble. To protect the seaways and defend against invasion from the English Channel, or the German North Sea, as it was known back then.

After the North Sea flooded the tide mill, our grandparents moved on. They lived for ten years and more at Hurst Farm at nearby Harking, Sussex. In labourers' cottages, numbered and rent paid. Aunt Francis Lucy, Father, Mark Henry, and eventually Aunt Mary, Aunt Ellen, and Aunt Marion lived in the cottage.

All the children attended the mill village school at Tide Mills. Marion, as the youngest, was still at home, on the day the census enumerator arrived in March 1871 to fill in forms with a portable desk setup and dip ink pen, as Father told us.

He liked this best, going to school and telling mother about this when he returned home tired and hungry!

Grandfather Mark Mepham, was by now, a journeyman miller, paid by the day. An itinerant worker, he moved around from place to place when needed and was paid for his work.

But grandmother Fanny and the children they stayed on, at the cottage at Hurst Farm. Through the winters, for many years, for the next year, they were tending the cows and sheep. Mending fences and walls, and preparing the fields for the next year's sowing and milling. The next year's harvest.

Our father, Mark, at eleven years of age, would be doing the same. On the day of the census in March 1871, so Father told us, a lady shareholder from Abingdon, Berkshire, was visiting Hurst Mill.

She and an engineer walked around the place with John Ticknall, a farmer of three hundred acres of mixed farming, corn and cows, and a watermill. The old mill at Hurst Green, was replaced soon after by a steam-powered mill.

Such machinery needed only one miller, and with fewer workers needed, our grandparents, with our father and our aunts, then, for want of work, they had to move on again.

For some time they settled at Uckfield, Sussex, along with the families of carters, cowmen, and sheepherders. By the village green, the corn mill, The Corn Mill public drinking house. The Holy Trinity church, and school.

With the children going to school, and in the summer to the seaside and funfair on the new pier at Brighton, these were happy days, as Father would tell us.

They later moved on again, and lived at Warren Mill, Withyam, East Grinstead, Sussex. Here there was a combined wind and water mill. The family lived on the mansion estate of farmer Ramsbotham, by the baronial Buckhurst Park and farm, Crowborough Manor House, and Little Windlesham, where Sir Arthur Conan Doyle lived.

Conan Doyle was a keen footballer, cricketer, and golfer, but is best known as the author of the *Sherlock Holmes* mysteries, and the Professor *Challenger* books. We read them all and knew those stories, so well. Remember our favourite: The Lost World?

That is what this world is became don't you think? Since the outbreak of war worlds are lost again. As we both will be someday, to this world, whatever happens?

Soon, grandfather was a miller again, in his own right, at the combined wind and watermill. In the summer, Father, like most agricultural children, worked for little or no pay in the fields and at the mill. With his parents, who were paid only meagre wages and all the grain they could take. Maybe, for porridge and baking cakes, or the gruel they would make—remember the gruel, Harry? When we could afford nothing else, they said it was good for us. It would keep us warm in the bitter-cold winter's morning, and when snow was on the ground.

Father went to school, as we did later, in London. Except when there was harvesting or other work to be done. He left school. Reading and writing well enough, and when he was thirteen, he left the mill for good.

Living and working away from home, as an indentured labourer, he was apprenticed into retail, at a shop on Vicarage Lane in Horley, Reigate, back in Sussex. The shop, where Father now also lived, stood alongside a row of farm cottages, the church and vicarage, and the shops of a butcher and a baker and, for all we know, a candlestick maker!:

Rub a dub dub

Three fools in a tub.

And who do you think they be?

The butcher, the baker,

The candlestick maker.

Turn them out, knaves all three!

Do you remember the nursery rhyme, Harry? Maybe that is us eh Harry? Knaves, all three of us, with our Father, and bless him too! The Saint Bartholomew's Church of England vicarage in Horley,

Sussex, had the luxury of a governess and cook, and possessed a kitchen garden and gardener's cottage.

This was from where our Father told us, that he would visit the Reverend Peter's family, discussing history, and disbursing religion, perhaps, which father had no time for.

With none of his own family around there, at the time. He would chat and do business, selling and buying the garden produce for the shop, and taking some to his own home, no doubt. And the children scrumping, from the garden. Later, in his early twenties, Father, lived alone off the High Street, Tenterden, back in Kent, where his father, and our grandfather were born.

With the family by then in Sussex, he visited them rarely due to his working days, one day a week to rest, and travelling by horse-cart or coach back then can you imagine! Father worked every day except Sunday, and could only visit on high days and holidays of which there were precious few.

He lived in his own rented cottage, alongside the low, white weather-boarded shop of Henry Boorman, of Hadlow Down, West Cross, Kent. Father was doing well in the retail trade. He was classed as a grocer with the Boormans' family, who were German, maybe, or Dutch.

In the shop, Father dressed in a grocer's green wide-striped apron with shirt and tie. Inside the shop were stacked sacks of grain and flour, locally milled perhaps, by our grandfather Mark Mepham!

Father would have been selling local farm produce and food-stuffs, along with that imported from elsewhere and everywhere, packaged and tin-canned. Home and Colonial.

It was a large, double shop Father worked in. As well as selling groceries, he also sold dress and suit cloth, hats, curtains, and pelmets. All kinds of furniture dressings were sold, all made to measure.

Father had broadened his skills and knowledge, and he became a draper's assistant. Now, he was dressed in clean white overalls over the suit and starched collar. He always wore to serve customers at The Moroccan Warehouse, in London later, do you remember that too? Father had no wife yet. Even though he had become a master grocer, draper, and milliner, no less, of the local Kent Wealds.

The trade in wool and collared dyed cloth was brought into the shop locally wind and water milled, and woven. As he would tell us, by father to be cut to size and pattern, tailored to fit; or sold-on, on rolls and bales.

England, then, was competing with the wool cloth and linen trade from Belgium at that time, and flax from over there, came from Flanders, and Holland. As is Kent and Sussex, another open, windy country, a land of high hills and watercourses full of ancient corn and cloth milling places.

Foreign cotton and local sheep and goats' wool delivered in bobbins and bundles to go to the mills locally, then sent and sold in shops in Kent and Sussex, and London, as cloth and clothes. There, in London, it was woven into fine garments for the fashionable West End department stores and displayed in the shop windows.

Father would soon anyway travel from the Kent and then Sussex North and South Downs. Through the village and small market town stations on the railway-line to Croydon and Putney. On the Surrey Thames River shore. Over the river to Middlesex (west) and eventually to the Middlesex (east) End of London, where, unbeknownst to him, our mother, Caroline Wells, then lived and worked, in service to a family of Importers, called Cotton.

Chapter 3: Mother's Family

Two years after the Battle of Waterloo and the Napoleonic Wars in Europe had ended in 1815, our maternal great-grandfather, mother's father John Coulthurst Wells, was born in Bethnal Green, Middlesex (East). A ne'er-do-well, it was said, he didn't go to school and didn't seem to work either, but he always had money; or so our Mother's family always said.

In his early twenties, John Coulthurst Wells classed himself a "traveller." Although it's far from certain exactly how far - if at all - he had actually travelled. His name, Coulthurst, is baronial, from South Yorkshire and East Anglia. There are North and South American settlers, named Coulthurst, too. He may have been the failed child of such a family. Left behind in Lincolnshire, perhaps to take the English-French feudal family name, and to then sully it, in London.

He must have been a rogue, a vagabond, an itinerant. As Grandfather Mepham was an itinerant miller, grandfather Wells, was an intinerant rogue. Later, staying at a boarding house in Brewer Street, between Piccadilly Circus and Leicester Square in the West

End of London.

John Coulthurst Wells lived in the shopping and theatre district, in one shared room of a narrow row of four-story stuccoed houses. The ground floors of which were converted into shops and stores - a watchmaker alongside a butcher and a home provisions store. Each storefront shared a narrow arch stone corner and possessed an open winding balustrade staircase.

The first floor held the largest rooms, for the shopkeeper's family. John lived above the baker's shop, in a small attic room, in a cramped garret. With a casement window looking out onto the back of the swish Savoy Hotel.

Below the stone window sill, and grubby brickwork, flames lit steaming underground kitchens, giving off flavours and fancy odours. Through the below ground pavement grilles, these warm vents were frequented by tramps and entire homeless families, often given the left-overs, hungry for food, as well as warmth, all day and night.

The winters could be very cold, and in summer, the sunshine hardly reached the pavement. Grandfather John Wells spent maybe two or three years there, huddled in front of a small coal fire, if any, kept awake by the noise from the nearby roads busy with horse and carriage and cart traffic all day and night.

However, a gentleman named Wells (not Coulthurst) did own property, on a corner of Golden Square, West One. This family apparently prospered, along with several of the same family name, earning a living as goldsmiths. John Coulthurst Wells may well have been trying to ingratiate himself to local goldsmiths of the same, Wells name.

John Coulthurst Wells shared rooms with a Suffolk baker, John Noiman, and returned home from the West End, disappointed, back in the East End, John Coulthurst Wells became a baker.

In those days, if you learned how to bake bread, and had a bread oven in which to bake, you could become a baker. John sold bread from his front room window. With it's Victorian drapery, if any, and he went out onto the street delivering, door to door.

Our mother's grandfather, John Coulthurst, met and married Harriet Tilbury, a dressmaker. John and Harriet lived at Providence Place, Bethnal Green. They lived with Harriet's family, her parents and eventually seven siblings; but then with Henry Ward, lodger, and a baker from Roysten, Cambridgeshire. John Coulthurst Wells and

Henry Ward, shared the rent of a bread oven in Bakers Rents, an alleyway off the road to Hackney. From the Thames Shore ditch, north to Islington, and south, and the new Liverpool Street Railway Station. With it's steam trains taking well-to-do passengers to the coast and seaside resorts. The cheapest Workmans, and the Seaside Trains, to Essex, and Kent, and for the hop picking. For the poor, as our mother's family were.

The family made their living now, as many others did, in the clothing trades, as house servants to the well-off; or now as irregular bakers. Sharing the cost of a sack of milled bread flour, yeast, and water, and the use of a kneading board and oven. Carrying trays of freshly baked bread and cakes on their heads, from the Baker's Rent, to the place of sale.

Soon, John and Harriet's eldest son, John, was born and died only of "the sickness" they were told, and hardly any mention made of it since. The next eldest, Uncle Arthur, was born soon after; and then the first girl, Aunt Harriet; and then Aunt Emily. The family moved around many times as the children grew up. Much as Father's family had done in Kent and Sussex, and they all got to go to the same Barnado's Copperfield Road Free School.

In amongst the warehouses of the Regent's Canal, from Paddington to King's Cross and Camden, Islington, north London. The Ragged Poor Schools, until the National Public School opened in St. Stephen's Road. Once Bow village, now Middlesex (east), London. Mother Caroline was born in 1865 at Old Ford, Bow Village, east of London,. At Middlesex (East) and brought up at 10 Beale Place.

A cobbled street cul-de-sac off the Hackney Road. Mother was brought up in Beale Place, by grandmother Harriet and her older brothers and sisters, our aunts and uncles. There were so many children, and when there was no longer room in the house. The older ones moved away, into service, or to marry and then if they could, started their own families, and our first cousins.

Our grandfather John Coulthurst Wells died by the time Mother was six years old, and she did not remember him much. Grandfather Wells wore long whiskers, she was told, though no beard or moustache.

Though she did not remember much of that really, Mother told us the stories of him anyway. When John Coulthurst Wells died, no one stayed to continue the bread-baking.

At home, at Beale Place, they lived and worked. Among silk-weavers: Huguenot refugees from France with French-sounding names and accents. Grandmother Harriet, who may have been French herself, was now a widow, and she worked at Beale Place winding cotton, freelance, you may say.

The youngest child, Uncle William, took up silk and cotton weaving from bobbins. For a young boy - under ten years - it was an arduous task, and noisy with the constant whirring of pattern looms. Aunt Emily, Mother's sister, and the next oldest at fifteen years, was a general servant living at home and bringing in pay.

Uncle Arthur Wells had left school at thirteen years. He was an errand boy, running deliveries and messages to and from the local shops and businesses for 'small pay'. All the children went to school. They must have attended the Ragged School or more likely the new National School on St. Stephens Road, and Beale Place, where others of the Well's then lived. The Wells' dropped the "Coulthurst" for reasons unknown; perhaps it was too difficult to spell, or even pronounce.

John and Harriet lived near the site of an old monastery, St. John on Bethnal Green, and the church house of Saint Paul's, on St.

Stephens Road. Some said, there was an ancient castle, where roamed the ghost of King John. The first and last John of England. King John managed to lose lands in western France, taken by conquerors and crusaders, back in olden times.

King John, was forced by the English barons to sign the Magna Carta in 1215. He had usurped the throne, and in turn was usurped by Richard the Lionheart, his French-speaking royal brother, on return from the Crusades in the Holy Lands of Palestine and the Turkish Ottomans.

By North Africa, where our Father, Mark Mepham, warehoused from Algeria and Morocco, Tangiers, and fought, perhaps almost died. On Richard's return, King John was deposed, and after taking refuge in Nottingham and London, east.

Via St Albans, and the Abbeys of Waltham and Barking, *up the Creek!* we would joke. King John, after French King Richard's departure to The Holy Land, seized the throne, supposedly went on to do battle with Robin Hood, and the poor of England.

If Robin Hood ever actually existed, that is.

We expect Robin Hood did exist in some way or form, but mostly because we want to believe. That King John, deposed, could have been seen in *ghostly* form as we played bows and arrows, along one of the walls of the so-called King John's Castle, at Old Ford. On the River Lea, or Lee Navigation, and Hertford Link to Paddington via Regent Park. One of the earliest canals in the land.

From the Thames docks in the east. To those in the west, via Paddington basin, to Thames Ditton and the Industrial north and east of England, Great Britain, and the Global Empire.

Do you remember playing with our cousins Henrietta (Etty), Clara, Harriet, and the others?

On the muddy unpaved streets of Bethnal Green and Bow, so-called the "rotten boroughs" for the corruption and poverty commonplace there. We played as children with our cousins who lived there, on our regular visits, down to the river Thames in the east, the East and West Hams, and the Abbey Mill, at a place called, Street, the river ford, at Stratford.

Where some other of our aunts and cousins' families also lived. Near to the great London Docks. The tidal Thames River running along by brick terraces and cobbled streets built and unbuilt lanes and alleyways where over the Docks, hung huge cranes winching on and off coal-fired steamships from the new Suez Canal.

Flowing with filthy mud into the river Thames. In the streets, horse droppings from the trade carts steamed and were scooped up and sold by anyone who would and for the small backyards and allotments the hundred year old Lee Navigation, one of the first or second in the country with lock gates and houses.

The Hertford and the Great Northern, and Grand Union canals. The men and horses led off loaded barges through Old Ford Lock, where we would watch them disappear up to Kings Cross and St. Pancras. On our north-east side of London, the other side, the south-easy Kent and Sussex, Surrey, and Paddington again.

From Waltham Abbey through Enfield and Walthamstow, the Hams and Barking by the creek; emptying River Lea into the Thames tidal river and docks. Tower Bridge and The Tower of London, we could visit. And the Kent shores moored there, across the waters, from across the sea.

Noisy and odorous, choking funnels blazed. Pouring smoke and steam over the streets of East and West Hams, by the Lea River and low marshes to the interior. Travelling through to the Paddington basin, in west London, from where we had visited for the day!

On the Lee Navigation and Hertford link. The Thames

riversides were rat-infested, pestiferous factories and tenements, hardly different in small-size and close-together, cutting out any sunlight, with rows of small windows, if any at all.

These factories and tenements were for large communities of itinerant and immigrant labourers from all over the world, or the Great Ships, and from all over the Empire. Sailors settled or moved-on. Those working in the so-called "base trades." Stayed.

Our cousin Mathilda, or "Milda" as she was known, lived with our grandparents John and Harriet even after Mother had left home to work at Hackney, and then Paddington in the west of London.

Milda was also a domestic servant, not living-in. She would walk daily to her place of employment, at one of the big houses in Hackney. She didn't go to school, any longer than she had to, left at thirteen years old, as did Mother. She left the overcrowded family home and was in service, too. Mother was living-in at the house of Mr. Daniel Pearson, vicar of St. James, in the ecclesiastical ward of St. James, the civil parish of St. John's, Hackney.

This was a wealthy suburb of professional people. Lawyers,

business people, and churchmen. The vicar's wife, Mary, was from the west country, Devon or Cornwall and almost fifteen years the vicar's junior.

Which was not unusual for the time, especially for the upper classes, rich merchants, vicar's wives and clergymen. Or, a warehouseman, and house live-in servant. Mary Pearson was a teacher and member of the Middlesex School Boards, and Mother may have taken lessons with her. As she learned to write and read, as did father, in the southern counties and now London retail trades; and as later, did we. You and me, Harry. Reading every and anything, we could get our hands on!

The vicar's family themselves, were from Surrey. Now, mother, living-in at 58 Kenninghall Road, Hackney. Mother was a domestic servant and living-in there since leaving school. Mother was a children's nurse, and served the religious family, along with the governess, another Harriet, from Berkshire, and Mary Pack, housemaid from Hampshire.

Mary Pack was a cook - from whom Mother learned something, no doubt - of those country parts then of Father's family.

The eldest of the vicar's ten children was called Mr. Henry

Pearson. A name Mother liked repeating with a fake upper-class posh (port out starboard home) accent, as in jest. Henry was an undergraduate at Oxford University, and a regular weekend visitor along with one Raoul de Bouble, a "continental name," Mother would say, using another funny fake accent, this time French.

As may be not so contrived, as her family were, likely Huguenot, and French themselves.

Raoul was a student at Aldershot, Hampshire. Attending the military college here, where I now write this, from the barracks and firing range.

In the knowledge I that we shall soon be set off from training to the real war.

To The Somme, most likely, and with you again, dear brother, Harry, short for Henry, Mark Henry! This other Henry, Henry Pearson, vicar to be, of St James, Hackney. He was studying religion at the college of divinity at Oxford, and they met. He and Raoul. Perhaps with the vicar of St. James, there and then, discussing together the ethics of training young men like ourselves.

Trained to fight and get killed in some Great War, as then for them yet to happen.

"Fighting and getting killed for what?" they may have asked, "God, King and Country?"

For Empire? For our Parent's, our Children, and our Children's children? For Their's? What and who are we fighting for now, in the end?

For our own lives and livelihoods - there is no doubt of that now; of that, there, is no doubt.

Chapter 4: Our Parents Meet

In 1891, when Mother was twenty-six, her services as a children's nurse were no longer required in the house at Hackney, and so she moved employment. She lived and worked at the house of Charlotte Cotton, a fifty-one-year-old widow, and her grown-up daughter at Warwick Road, Paddington, West London.

The late Mr. Cotton hailed from the county of Norfolk. Mrs. Cotton was now living on her own means, and perhaps the family's wealth had originally come from the cotton trade, as their name. Built on slavery abroad and indentured labour at home cotton then as now shipped via India and America to the river ports and canals of London and Liverpool, and on to the factory mills all over the north of England. contributing greatly to the wealth of the still Great British Empire.

As for the family, whether Cotton was their original name or not, it certainly defined the family's position and purpose in life. They had made their name speculating on one shipment, perhaps, across and back across the great Atlantic Ocean.

Either from the former American colony or the colonies of

the Far East, and from that profited, and made more as such, each future time cash crop. Cotton came from India through Egypt and the Suez Canal - opened in 1869, and a wonder of the world we saw in pictures at the museum.

Perhaps the cotton was taken through the Regent's Canal and overland by horse and camel drawn the same cotton silk Mother Caroline's family would wind at home in Beale Place.

Finding it's way eventually as clothing and drapery, in the prestigious London warehouses, and department stores. Those Grand Stores sold everything. From clothing, to foreign carpets and furniture.

From Morocco, through France or around the Bay of Biscay. To the docks at Bristol and Liverpool, and the south-coast. The English Channel, to ports in Sussex and Kent, and along the Thames, to the London Docks.

Many of the large houses and small shops and buildings in Oxford Street, had been joined-up and made into shopping galleries and restaurants. Like Paris, or New York, maybe. Along Oxford Street, owned or in trust to the University. Where *in much older times* prisoners were once taken from the French Conqueror's Tower of London.

Or to Newgate Prison, to be hanged or drawn and quartered for their crimes.

This road now Oxford Street, named by Oxford (University where mother may have gone "for a day out" she would joke) with brand new buildings gifted, owned, and so built. These large warehouses and department stores replaced the small country shops, with their Dickensian Olde Curiosity Shoppe broad curved Bottle-Bottom windows, and wide doors. Transformed into larger, grander buildings. Their upstairs quarters gilded, are as if gutted, by fire or demolition inside, and roofs joined together outside along the pavements and new roves, and beams and pillared archways and Arcades, like Burlington Berties', to hold the weight.

As if from Chaucer to Shakespeare, Austin to Dickens, these were Old Curiosity Shops, along to Fleet Street and the Courts of Law. The new Department Stores, from Colonial Great British Isles, America, and all sorts of other parts, Indian Raj's and African Kings and Queens, were given large windows and gallery floors filled with everything. Delights from the Empire, British, and Father's exotic French Morocco.

Brought from afar, from the coast and countryside along the Kent and Sussex Trade Roads. From Hampshire and the Surrey-shore. And then, for people to wander around and view.

Around Piccadilly Circus, and the shops and theatres and music halls where John Coulthurst Wells roamed. There were tearooms, and public liquor houses. The Cottons, Mother said, would call for a carriage to take them anywhere. Some of the neighbours in Warwick Road even had their own coachman and stabled horse.

These were the professional classes, arts and craftspeople living along there. A house furnisher, a silver and heraldic engraver. A printer, and a barrister of law from South America. Mother would mimic them, too, speaking with a not-so-familiar Spanish or Portuguese accent.

There was a small private church school with a chaplain, and Boarding Houses serving several Clerks at the London Stock Exchange. They all had their domestic live-ins, as mother was. There was a retired pharmacist and others living on their own means with their small families and domestic servants.

Mrs. Cotton's daughter in the house at Warwick Avenue, was

the same age as Mother. Mid-twenties, although I suppose they conversed little. 'Lizard' Cotton, for that was her name, apparently, was an actress, and acted, or attened the theatres in the West End of London. Born in Africa, as of some colony, don't know which. She may have been intentionally named, as the Cotton family itself.

'There are many lizards abroad, in the hotter climes…' or so Father told us. Or maybe there was an error of transcription from the census of 1891 - Liza, perhaps? Anyway, as Mother said, "Lizard" suited her better!

There was even an exotic ostrich feather and umbrella - and glove-manufacturing company. German-owned, would you have it - in Warwick Road! And closed, like the Moroccan Warehouse, at the commencement of hostilities, in 1914. The Moroccan Goods Warehouse would close at the start of hostilities; and where Father then worked. Moved up from Kent, Sussex, and Surry, over the Thames river to Paddington, west London. Mother was living-in as a domestic servant in Paddington, west-London. Where many poorer east-Londoners, English, Scots, Welsh and Irish, and other Great British, and from far abroad, lived, and also worked.

And it was there she met Mark Henry Mepham.

Mother might have seen Father there, or he saw her when the Cotton family were out buying additional accoutrements for their already elaborately and over furnished home, reminders they would have cherished, perhaps of Africa, America or the Indies, and Colonial times.

Or, perhaps, Father was delivering to the Warwick Road by cart and horse or maybe, by then, motor lorry. Mother would have been walking back along one of the swish side roads of South Kensington.

Returning from shopping for the family with the cook, Sarah Olive from Sussex, who she told us, taught mother to cook soups and stews. As we were brought up on, and roast meat and gravy on Sunday, and Christmas. Sarah Olive and Mark Henry Mepham had something in common, and they talked together about Sussex. But it was Caroline who Father was to court, marry, and have two sons by.

Caroline Wells and Mark Henry Mepham married in 1891, and Mother became Caroline Mepham. They lost a male child at birth, in London, the year before you, Harry Arthur, were born at Droxford, Hambledon, Hampshire, in the summer of 1895.

At our grandparents, Mark and Fanny, living, and working at

a grand old age, water mills on the rivers of Hampshire. There were still bread-flour mills on the nearby River Hamble. Which flows into the Solent, between the English Channel and the Atlantic Ocean, and the troop-carrying Navy ports of Portsmouth and Southampton.

After losing her first child - and as our maternal grandparents John and Harriet in Bethnal Green had also died. Mother went to stay with the Mepham grandparents Fanny and Mark, in the Hampshire countryside until you, Harry, were born.

Mother told us she enjoyed the fresh air, being away from the London smog and fog. Expecting another child - you, Harry Arthur. Mother wanted to make sure you would survive.

She was looked after by our grandparents, Fanny and Mark there, while Mark Henry and Caroline, were now living in Paddington, Middlesex.

Father, Mark Henry remained behind, when you were born, Harry, for work at the stockroom, and deliveries from the Morocco Warehouse.

Wages to feed and house the family, and family to become. In the row of four-story terraced townhouses, with bay windows, front steps, and three rooms on each floor. They rented the first floor at 56 Walterton Road. I was named Walter, after the street we lived in. Having survived birth there, us both having survived birth.

Various tradesmen and their families lived on each of the Landings of 'Our House'. The townhouse had an indoor staircase and a fire escape at the back leading down to a small paved yard. How we loved playing on that escape and on the steps in front of the house, in the street where there were mainly horse-drawn coaches then. That were the more dangerous than the occasional motor vehicle chugging along, barely moving.

Slower than us children running alongside. It could be dangerous: Many deaths were caused on the roads with horse-cabs, trams and omnibus, and brand new cars, going so fast, rattling noisily past. Even when we were told not to, we would venture out.

On the top floor of our house was a watchmaker who used the better light up there to work. Next, there was a lead-worker and a plumber and roofer, who came and went smelling of oil and metal.

We were on the first floor from the ground. The spiked railings at the front were removed when the war started, to be melted down for weapons. 'Lock Stock and Barrel!' as we would say. In the basement below us lived an old army officer, retired, pensioned.

A veteran, we were told, of the 1865 Crimean War, in Russia. Do you remember that poem of Tennyson's we were all taught to recite at school about that?

The Charge of the Light Brigade. "Into the valley of Death / Rode the six hundred."

Only a few, like Father, still with his gentle rural accent, were from the English countryside. None was from the East End of London like Mother, with her sharp, cockney tongue.

We heard many accents from all over the European and Colonial worlds, as we do, here; there. France again, the Western Front. As you would tell us, Harry, and you and Mother would mimic the accents of Australia, Africa, the Americas India and Ceylon.

The far (from us) and mid-East of The World, to us. Living all together, happy and sad and happy again, all the time. Each landing of that building, built to last, had three rooms including their own kitchen extension with a shared toilet and washroom, and backstairs to a small yard.

At the front, steep steps led down to the narrow pavement and wide road where you and I, Harry, we would play. Along the front and corner walls we fought each other.

As brothers do, playing make-believe games and war games with the other children. Even then, only one of us could have survived. Grandfather Mark Mepham worked on an ancient water mill, before he died.

At Hambledon, in this same county of Aldershot, Hampshire, aged sixty-five years, in 1896. You, Harry Arthur, were nearly four years old when I, Walter, was born in the warm spring of the year; and in the late winter cold of that same year 1898. Grandmother Mepham died, also "of the sickness" and was buried with Grandfather Mark, in the churchyard, at Uckfield, Sussex, England.

The house and first upper floor, at 56 Walterton Road, Paddington,

where Walter Mepham was born.

Part Two: For or Against

Chapter 5: Conan Doyle

France, September–October, 1917

Dear Harry, from 1906, throughout the Great War, and until his death at Windlesham, Sussex, in 1930, the well-known Scot (from German Georgian Edinbugh) Sir Arthur Conan Doyle lived at Crowborough, Sussex. The epitaph on his tombstone there reads, "Steel true, blade straight, knight, patriot, physician and man of letters," and sums him up.

From Windlesham Manor, Crowborough, Conan Doyle raced cars before the Great War, and supported the building of a tunnel between France and England. To avoid being cut off from food and supplies, in case of any conflict. He had seen the build-up of the German navy in the Baltic, and the development of tanks and airplanes for military purposes, and he warned against the possible attrition of the English seaways by the new German U-boat and submarines.

Conan Doyle started calling this war "The Great War" before it had even begun.

He regarded the coming conflict as inevitable. He took part in the Prince Henry of Prussia Cup. The international road competition against the Germans ran from Hamburg to London, and each car carried a military observer from the opposite team. There was hostility growing, even then. With Conan Doyle and his beloved wife, Jean Leckie driving in 1911, the British team won.

The British Bentley outdid the German Mercedes-Benz. Conan Doyle and Jean, along with their automobiles, crossed the English Channel on board the paddle steamers from Newhaven or Portsmouth.

At the age of fifty-five in 1914, Conan Doyle was rejected for service abroad, and instead organized the Home Guard. His unit became the Crowborough Company of the Sixth Royal Sussex Volunteer Regiment. When offered the command position in the new battalion, Conan Doyle refused. He wanted to show his countrymen that all were equal in the defence of Britain, and he entered the group as a private.

He volunteered Home Guard, at the Crowborough Army Camp that he established, in the grounds. Resting and feeding the troops, in training before their nineteenth birthdays, then on their way to the south coast ports, and on to Western Front.

From Windlesham Manor, in 1917, Sir Arthur Conan Doyle wrote that he could hear the sound of the cannon and machine gun from The Somme across the English Channel. As did Prime Minister Lloyd George, who was famously said to have heard the guns from his office in Downing Street, London.

Whether Lloyd George was speaking metaphorically, as if he could have heard them. David Lloyd George had cautioned his government, not to announce the true numbers of dead and wounded, from the Somme, Passchendaele and Ypres. As the people would not accept the war. They would reject it and refuse to fight on. The peace cry would get louder, and the pressure to sue for peace, stronger.

We needed to be seen winning the war, in the hope the other side would capitulate, with a retreat, armistice, and Peace Treaty, like that of Versailles, between the French and Prussians in 1871.

By the time the Great War started in 1914, most agreed with Conan Doyle, and Winston Churchill, First Lord of the Admiralty, that not only had war been inevitable, but that it had also become unavoidable.

Where you, Harry, have been. With nothing to show, but the

dead and wounded. Few returned home alive or dead, from those places. And that is where I will be heading, no doubt, by the time I am nineteen years, and a day!

The lanes and roads became busier in those days with farm traffic - horse-drawn carts and a few motor tractors, motorcars, and lorries - and then also the marching of feet, and troop carriers onward toward the coast. Toward France and the battlefront. The Crowborough camp is where our father, Mark Henry, passed through in 1915 to serve at Gallipoli, Turkey; as you, Harry Arthur, in the same year, to the Somme and Ypres; and I, soon now, to serve at

France, as we are now told.

Plaque at 2 Upper Wimpole Street, Marylebone,Midds. (west) dining club. ACD worked and wrote here in 1891. Below: Early 1900 Crowborough Camp

1915 (below):

2nd London Infantry Brigade   Camp Hill. Crowborough

Chapter 6: Lord Bertrand (Bertie) Russell

We moved residence from 56 Walterton Road, to Coptic Street buildings, Holborn, London. Which had a WC1 (West Central) postal code, making it West London. Even though it is East of the city, and to the North.

We moved there because our parents could no longer afford the rents in Maida Vale, Kensal Green, now The City of Westminster (North). 1965 and no longer Middlesex, but Greater London.

The housing our parents could afford was in Stedham Chambers, Holborn and St. Pancras, UK Parliamentary constituency, London Borough of Camden, Hampstead, and Barnet ceremonial assembly Middlesex. And then the Austinian Hills and large Country Houses of Hertfordshire.

Near to the British Museum, we lived, and from there father would walk to work, along Coptic Street, to Tottenham Court Road, and along Oxford Street. There was going to be a great depression, some warned, and things were difficult.

Eventually, father lost his job at The Moroccan Warehouse, and the Import Trade halted. Went out of business, due to the coming

'Great War'; and the two preceding Morocco Crisis'. Morocco and Algiers for France and Spain. For us British: Egypt and Palestine controlled areas.

The German Kaiser ejected from Morocco, supporting the Sultan and Egypt. Between Italy and Turkey, a war, and the German gun-ship Panther outside French Agadir, 1911. In Palestine, and Syria and the Arab peninsular. The Germans, and the Belgian King Leopold wanted Empire in Africa, and attacked the Congo of French Africa, in such a bid, and required safe passage through the English Channel, back to the North German Sea. War would ensue.

But for now, instead of two rooms, we now lived in three. The new building's apartments were constructed with tall chimneys where decorative red brickwork swirling like the wind, forming ears of corn and figures of birds: cranes and storks. Inside there was a courtyard with open, shared balcony walkways of reinforced concrete and wrought iron; and a communal lawn and garden below, where you could meet others in pleasant surroundings, and go about your business.

Stedham Chambers (above). Below, blue plaque Bertrand Russell
1892-1970 Philospher and campaigner for peace lived here 1911-16.

Cobbled alleyways took you to the busy paved streets and the salubrious surroundings. Which included interesting shops and cafes. I wondered if we moved there because it was called Stedham Chambers. Stedham is a well-known and picturesque place in Sussex, with a manor house and water mill. It may just have reminded Father of who he was and where he was born. He might have liked to visit there again someday.

The Stedham Chambers, Holborn, was built and named by a family of Sussex grocers who sold up and made good, in the Convent Gardens, and at Spitalfields, east of the city. The fruit and vegetable and flowers and fish markets.

Our rooms were opposite the dairy at Pied Bull Court and Yard, where milk churns were brought in from the dairy farms in Middlesex, Hertfordshire, and Essex. We lived among the service workers employed in the markets, and the Grand Houses and University Colleges, at Cambridge Circus.

The School of Oriental and African Studies was nearby. As well as the British Museum we would visit, with father and mother worked. We would talk about all The Treasures of History, therein. There was a connection with North Africa, and The Morocco

Warehouse, where Father worked. Before this Great War he was then *top* salesman.

He needed to know about the items he was selling, specialising in the exotic furniture and ornaments, carpets and cloths of Morocco where he wished he would be able to visit someday.

He would take us to visit the warehouse, and the museum. From six years to thirteen we both went to the National School nearby, where we learned to read and write, and we did well.

We liked our history, and took after our father in that way. I had a job as a newsboy, as well, selling newspapers and calling out the headlines to passers-by on the corner of New Oxford Street.

Then, I joined Barclays Bank in The City, clerking. You, Harry, were good at numbers too, and became a bookmaker's clerk at the Sporting Club, the gambling club and casino favour whose doors opened onto the corner of Tottenham Court Road and Oxford Street opposite the Shaftesbury Theatre, and was favoured by the toffs and rich foreigners.

There were a few famous people around the place: actors and writers called "The Bloomsbury Set".

At the time, one of the Set was Lord Russell, otherwise

known as Bertrand "Bertie" Russell, a famous mathematician and philosopher. An atheist and a pacifist, Russell moved into the nearby Russell Chambers, built and named by his formerly aristocratic family, offering basic accommodation for the poorer professionals and academics of the London University colleges.

Russell, who was well-known for his anti-war sentiments, lived at number 32 Russell Chambers. He wrote pamphlets and books about his beliefs, spoke about them, lost his job at Cambridge University, and even went to prison because of views of war and this Great War in particular.

Russell didn't join the Public Schools and University Men's Force, commissioned as officers in 1915. Russell said it was a war of imperialism. Even if the Kaiser had already moved into the Netherlands and Belgium, heading for France and the English Channel, he still believed an invasion of England was unlikely. Most people, however, including Conan Doyle, disagreed with Russell, insisting we had to go to war.

It was preferable to sue for peace, Russell argued, preferable to go for early appeasement, which is what the Kaiser wanted as well apparently, but we were not told this until afterwards.

Peace was what the German people, especially the workers, and the soldiers by implication, and conscription, wanted too. It was what the British may have wanted if we were asked.

We might have accepted peace, since we, or they, surely did not want the Great War, either. Even if we did lose our sea power and our Empire that was just what this war was all about: the prestige and power and jealousy of the rulers.

There was nothing for us, the people, to gain from it. Russell said that meeting force with force was wrong and two wrongs did not make a right. Fighting fire with fire was stupid, when a bucket of water was required.

A war of offense, even as defence, was not justified, Russell said, because of the horrors war brought. Each side setting out to annihilate the other, without remorse or remedy.

"Hatred, by a tragic delusion, perpetuates the very evils from which it springs," Russell wrote.

Here at the front, that is just what it is: Kill before you get killed.

Well, we never think we ourselves are going to be killed, do we? Always dream, and hope to return in one piece, at least.

Yet, we always know it could be any of us, anytime. In the end, there did not seem to be a choice. It was paid work, of a sort, for our families when there was not a lot of work available. Crash of a different sort. The money supply. Gold Stocks were talked about. Unemployment. Not enough to pay the workers. Not enough to spend, on anything. Rent and food.

So, to become military-heraldic. For, The Bank of England, Scotland, Wales and Ireland. For the fighters, as for the objectors, it was never really going to be glorious.

Workers and soldiers at the newsstand on New Oxford Street. The City bowler hatted gentlemen and office boys talked about these choices, or decisions. If that was what they were: to fight or not to fight, and for what?

For whom? Against what? Against whom? The whole world? This is a World War soon enough: the Great War. Bertrand Russell and Conan Doyle corresponded regularly on the subjects of life after death, and spiritualism. Atheism, and Communism, as being talked about in Russia. Heaven or Hell?

Some of this was written up in the newspapers I was selling, and reading them at the same time!

Conan Doyle was agnostic and a transcendentalist, believing a greater truth was somehow out there.

Russell was an atheist rationalist idealist. A logician and mathematician, believing only reason can point to the truth. Their debates were repeated on the streets of London, and everywhere else literate people congregated.

Sometimes as rowdy mobs, including at the newspaper stand. Outside of Parliament and at street corners and workplaces. Trades Unions were on the rise. Speaking off of soap box stands, shouting and arguing. Eventually Russell and Conan Doyle fell out over the question of an afterlife, life after death, and no longer communicated.

I do wonder how they feel about that question now?

Coming into 1917, with so many dead, that we could not help but know about, but chose to believe. Believe there were only many rather than a quarter, half, in the first battles lost, with no gain of ground. Stalemate trench warfare.

Conan Doyle subscribed to the Society for Psychic Research, whose members attempted to prove communi-cation from beyond the grave. Through spiritual contact. By "automatic" or "spirit" writing and other means.

But what would the fallen say now?

What would they…what would we - you and I - say now?

Russell was in Cambridge police-cells, and later Brixton prison, for 'passive resistance to military or naval service', ironically, for Breach of the (alleged) Peace. Treason, almost, for proposing a peace.

Russell held that there was no life after death. He said all was obtained in the here and now. Through the faculty of reason, and that we held a moral responsibility, individually and collectively, for either and both. The existence of Heaven on Earth, or the unleashing of Hell on Earth.

The question that ultimately divided them was whether to go to war with Germany, and with our Allies Russia and France and Belgium, with the Entente Cordiale already signed-up.

Whether going to such a war was a good thing or a bad thing. A just war, or not? Is any war just? Is reneging on cordial agreements, made many years before, in 1907. Was this just, or the only reason for such bloodshed?

Conan Doyle would say yes, it was necessary. Russell would

say it was up to every individual to decide for him, and herself, whether to fight or not, in a righteous war.

Russell believed conscription was wrong, and that was the real issue. The war may be right or wrong...

What mattered was how many believed it was right, or wrong. How many felt this worth fighting for? They who would actually fight? On either, or both and any side?

They all would have their rational reasons, for or against. They would all be different, in some way or another. But, in the end, it came down to each of us having to decide for ourselves. We were told we had to fight to avoid blockade and invasion, from the English Channel and the so-called North German Sea.

France, the ports in Belgium, and the colonies all over the world were the prizes worth fighting for. Here on the Western Front, soon; and the free passage of trade, from the Atlantic, and World, lest England be starved into submission.

If we survived, or even if we died; we would be pensioned so our families, our children - if we had any - and our children's children could continue in freedom and peace. This was The War to

End All Wars, we were told, and we would be able to give life, for All Our descendants.

And that is why we are out here now, fighting in these killing fields.

Chapter 6: Arthur Wells

It was not that far from west to east London.

Paddington to Bethnal Green and Old Ford. You could do it by barge, along the canal, but we would take the omnibus to Old Ford. Then, Bethnal Green.

Then over Tower Bridge, or through the new Rotherhithe Tunnel. Under the Thames, to the New and Old Kent Roads

Toward the end of every summer we would visit our mother's brother, Arthur Wells, and all our Wells relations living in the village sprawl of the overcrowded East End of London.

From there, we would go down to Father's Kent countryside, for the hop-picking season. Some walked all the way, while others, like us, took buses and trains to the southward-facing rolling hills of the Kent and Sussex Downs. Danes, from the sea.

Where the Britain and Anglo-Saxons met the late Roman conquerors, and the French Normans. Planted vineyards, producing wine right up to the end of the seventeenth century, when Samuel Pepys was writing his diary of London life.

By the time you and father, and then myself, travelling

south, to Europe, the summers were shorter and colder, and faster-ripening hops were grown, instead. For adding to the traditional English and British ales, and they have been ever since.

These Beer-Hops had to be picked, of course, and wouldn't pick themselves. And so doing, gave us a taste of the sort of country life Father must have lived as a young and unattached suitor to Caroline Wells.

Up to 1914 itself, for a few weeks of every summer, the Wells and Mepham families gathered together to work. Sometimes, for a month or more picking hops and cutting them down for the next year. While the adults worked, we children amused ourselves with hop battles.

One of us would throw a hop, others would join in, and then we had a war! We played around between the rows of huts where we slept, cooked, and ate, and had to be quietened down to sleep. Every evening we sat up late, while the adults drank beer, smoked cigarettes, and talked outside.

We enjoyed those days with Uncle Arthur and Mother's family. Seven years older than Mother, Uncle Arthur could not write his own name, or at least that's what Mother told us. It was why she was always so adamant that we go to school, and learn to read, write, and do sums.

Uncle Arthur put a cross on the marriage certificate when he married Aunt Clara (Wilson), from Carlisle. Uncle Arthur could not read words very well, but was a virtuoso by the fact that he could sight-read music. He played the violin, viola, and violin-cello.

He also had a mechanical piano player with the tough paper rolls scored, and played for the notes. The music was played by the moving of foot-pedalled levers. He would pump the pedals for accompaniment, hammering at the keys, and play along on the violin, or cello, both hands and feet occupied.

He would be half-turned to the room full of relatives, neighbours, and friends.

His audience sang along and danced on the unvarnished wooden planks, uncarpeted floor, like the trenches we start to dig.

Uncle Arthur obtained his best violin, viola, and violoncello from Aunt Clara, who had connections in the millinery and furniture trade! Aunt Clara, had been apprenticed at fourteen years, making musical instruments, in one of the furniture factories along the Lee Navigation canal. Up and down, to and from, the famous gunpowder mills at Barking Creek and Waltham Abbey, nearby, the Lee-Enfield Rifle Works, up river, at Enfield Lock. Where barges were pulled along the canals by unshoed horses, for fear of a spark. As we may be affeared out here, now.

Where our rifles here at the front are meticulously manufactured, and brought out to us. Shipped and by the horse-drawn cartload as along the metalled army roads, from the back trenches. Uncle Arthur had a horse and cart. To transport his similarly meticulously woodworked and upholstered furniture about.

Then, from St. Stephens Road, Bow, rather than facing the expense of hiring a cart or a lorry as some did, they would go down to Kent on their own horse and cart.

They worked together, Arthur and Clara, fully self-sufficient, they would say, of their own means. They grew fruit and vegetables at their garden allotment, and in the yard at the back, where the horse would be stabled. Through the gateposts around the side of the house, and leaving its manure for their garden!

We discovered it could also be collected in the family garden pail, taken out, and sold on, money earned, given straightaway, to Aunt Clara, some for sweets, to the corner shop with our cousins. Do you remember, Harry? Aunt Clara, must have done all the reading and writing, all the paperwork.

They lived and worked together as cabinetmakers and upholsterers - now the Wells family business, in St. Stephens Road, Bow. They bought and brought their wood and materials along the River Lea and Lee Navigation, imported cargoes of materials and wood, coal and pig iron for iron-welding fireplaces and building furniture, bricks and glass windows for the houses.

From Kent and Sussex, the northern coastal traffic, and boats and ships from all over the World.

The gunpowder was brought down from the northern nitrate mines where plentiful urine had been previously shipped, 'taking the piss', to be added to charcoal, and sulphur brimstone.

Now this was brought along the Thames and Lea Valley. To Barking, and from Waltham Mills. Iron smelted and copper from the Walthamstow copper mills. To make cartridges, safely sealed, and ready to kill. Arthur and Clara, may have turned out furniture, fixtures, and fittings for the Palaces and Grand houses that were occupied for the London Season. Of the royalty and aristocracy and other hangers-on in those days. For the dances and balls which became fashionable for the burgeoning professional classes, of the inner workhouses, and outer leafy Epping Forest.

Now in Leyton and the Walthamstow village suburbs. By the Imperial Piano Company at Leyton, Essex, on the other bank of the Lea Valley. Where our Uncle Henry Stow, of Walthamstow! Worked; and got Arthur Wells the shifting jobs, no doubt.

Urban and urbane, Uncle Arthur and Aunt Clara lived and worked, at St. Stephens Road, Bow. Close to the cottages at 10 Beale Place, where Grandmother Wells had lived; and at 19 Beale Place, where our cousins spun silk and cotton. Arthur and Clara moved from Beale Road, to the tidy terrace in Bow by the long Roman Road Street Market, and their well appointed terraced house and yard.

This was where the horse stuck its head through the kitchen window, over the butler's sink in the back-scullery, and knocked plates and cutlery off the shelf to general pandemonium! Do you remember that? I do, or at least think I do! What a commotion! Or so we were told...

They were wonderful days, weren't they, Harry Arthur? Of our other cousins our age, there was Florrie, Clara Eleanor, Gracie, Emily, and Charles who died of tuberculosis. Then our cousin Etty, for Henrietta - another French name.

Because of their names, I often wonder if the Wells were French. William and Harriet were French Christian Protestant Huguenot refugees, that took up home, and cottage silk-weaving trade, to the east end of London, and with noticeable names to match; then again, the William, Mark, and Henry, and Harriet, perhaps back to the invasion of 1066, and all that.

Of mothers cousin's, sixteen years older than Mother, Henrietta Wells, or Etty married, Alf Byfield in 1908. At the civil parish church of St. John's, Hackney Road. Where Mother once worked for the churchman, and might even have set up the wedding for them at a discounted price, as with the furniture for the house, bought through someone known, in the trade.

It was a grand do, that wedding, by all accounts.

Mother's family, were the Wells's, and who married into the Byfield's, both of Walthamstow, Winifred Byfield, and Albert Stow, of Walthamstow. Albert married Winnie Byfield, from St. Elizabeth Road, off of the same 113 Higham Hill Road, London, where Albert was also brought up; and near enough to the Blackhorse Road School, where they first met, unknowingly sat together in a school photo. They courted after meeting at the Workers Education Drama Class on Greenleaf Road, and the school that they attended,

Blackhorse Road school, had a catchment area not at Queen Elizabeth Road, but Forest Road, Walthamstow, to Essex, and the countryside beyond.

In which case would they ever have met? Married, and had children, our cousins? Win and Bert travelled into London as regularly as they could afford, to attend promenade concerts at the Royal Albert Hall, Wigmore Hall, and smaller lunchtime concerts at St Johns' Smith Square.

Wins' family were from 8 Farnborough Avenue, off Forest Road, before they moved to the new houses being built in Guildford Road, Walthamstow, on the edge of the Epping Forest. Alf Byfield, was a glazier who worked on all the new housing estates being built on the grounds of the large houses and farms and fields in Walthamstow.

Alf also moonlighted as a violinist in the orchestra pit in the new cinema at the top of the High Street, on Hoe Street. I wonder if they got free seats 'on the house' from Alf? Did he get that pianola from the Leyton Piano Works, where he would get capentered fancy woodwork to make into his own furniture, and shared with the newly wedded, the writing desk, hall stand, and full-sized wardrobes, made to measure. Whenever anyone became married, eh! He played the violin and pianola (mechanical piano), singing, bawdy or otherwise, rustic songs, and EastEnd Music Hall, at the same time, probably.

Albert would have played Church Music from the Baptist Church opposite 113. He learned Classical, and Music-Hall, while at the Stow family home, father Henry Stow, and Albert in his later years, plink plonked tunes to sing and dance to, once the carpet was rolled back, of a weekend, regular dance parties, playing the dodgy pianola.

Installed at 117 Higham Hill Road. Mortgaged on the Royal Navy wages of Great Uncle Harry, while at sea, First World War. I must say that I was not given very regal forebears, but I was not able to raise any objection at the time.

At that time many children suffered similarly from poverty, and war, and faced the perils of both from the day they were born.

Apart from The First World War, well and truly started at that time, the other perils in that little bedroom at 15 St Stephens Road, Walthamstow, were in a framed family photograph enlargement hanging at a later date, on the wall of the living room at 113 Higham Hill road, where we moved to soon after I was born (the picture sadly lost, except in my memory (see later family various throughout this book Sarah, Henry, Bella, Harry, Agnes Archie and Albert…).

In that photograph were the next youngest member of the family, my older brother, Archie (b.1905). Archie's education was interrupted by the war, his prospects much reduced. The other brother Harry (b.1900) was a very tall man in naval uniform. He signed up to the Royal Navy early in the war, to escape derision from local girls, who thought him older than he was.

His ship was torpedoed (Atlantic, out of Portsmouth) all escaped except another lad my brothers age, who died sadly, from a broken neck.

Then there was my big sister Bella (Isabella Rose b. 1899), known familiarly as Bella. She was fairly tall, well proportioned, and good looking. Very authoritive, but kind. Her life was affected by a tragic incident in her childhood. It happened on a Xmas eve (1904) in the little cottage on St Stephens Road where I was born (off Grove Road, Walthamstow and Whipps Cross Road, Leyton, on the borders of Epping Forest, Essex).

Mother (Sarah (nee Scott) b.1873 Lambeth) was busy cooking, and she, Bella, around five years, was told to take a lighted candle upstairs to bring granddad James Scott (b.1829 Tynemouth, Northumberland, widower of Elizabeth (nee Peacock) of Darlington) down stairs, to have his evening meal.

Now, to go upstairs in that small cottage you had to open a

door, next to another door to the pantry cupboard. Inside the staircase door there was a very steep staircase. At one point on the

way down granddad

lost his footing, Bella was unable to support him so he fell down the stairs and broke his neck.

It seems the end was quite peaceful according to mother, he knew he was near the end. Mother said a little prayer, and he died in her arms. Mother never made any reference to it in Bella's presence thereafter, and they were very fond of each other.

Consequently she, Bella, became very religious and serious, and although she did have a sense of humour, she did make me take church seriously, although I did sometimes forget to say my prayers! She had a good soprano voice for hymn singing. Bella did very well at school for those days, and got a year or two's extension at school, to 15 years. Her one and only gentleman friend was one Will Reynolds, who treated me very well. When she left school she became a shirt machinist, and finished up in management at Achilles Serres, on Billet Road (above).

Where there was the Blackhorse Road Station (moved from one side of the railway bridge to the other on Blackhorse Road. From where Aunt Clara Wells living with Etty and Alf, her eyesight failing her. Aunt Clara and Win went to work ar Paquin's dressers to the French milliners, in the department stores, upstairs, at the back of the large premises, in the West End of London. Where the clothes of the rich and well-known, were sewn.

Aunt Clara may have lost her sight completely, anyway. But with Phyllis, Wins sister working as a nursery nurse, they helped bringing up the four niece and nephews, when Clara retired early, and received a government pension.

Albert and Win were married, at St. Johns in Walthamstow, a large edifice on the Chingford Road corner, of St. Johns Road. According to the photographs taken with the phosphorous flash-camera at the photographic studio on Kingsland Road, Hackney, and as for our cousin Clara and Uncle Arthur's wedding, in 1908.

There was a beautiful lace and silk dress made by family, and no doubt people they knew, they moved to live in rent at Marlborough Avenue, Chingford. Rented upstairs as the next in Beech Hall Road, where Great Uncle Alf to be, had glazed the windows, and received a suitable mortgage from his work, to start to buy in instalments.

Aunt Clara, and Arthur, in the skilled millinery, and furniture, and carrying trades. We Men in tailored suits, with bow ties hired for the men; and us lads at the time in long socks over our knees!

Uncle Alf Byfield, was against, but Uncle Arthur Wells supported The Great War, from the start. From before the start. He said there were always those who did not support war under any circumstances.

He was too old to sign up anyway, but by 1914, at fifty-eight, married late, Uncle Arthur kept the horse and cart at 101 St. Stevens Road, Bow, for any war service as may be required.

Our aunts in Bow continued weaving, knitting, and sewing, now making the uniforms for the troops. Other women were working in munitions in the Barking Creek factories, and up the Lee Navigation at the Royal Enfield works.

The Women were doing everything the men who were not there, could do. Casting iron and steel, by furnace and lathe workshops, filing to the correct millimetre, and then packing the bullets and shells, into boxes and wooden crates to be sent out here to the Western Front.

Uncle Arthur and Aunt Clara's terraced house in St. Steven's Road, had a back room and kitchen scullery beyond the front room. There were two or more rooms upstairs, and outside were shared water taps and toilets, with the whole row.

Our cousins got married and moved out, or to go into service. Clara and Uncle Arthur had lodgers, to pay for their premises they continued to work out of, on their own account. The lodgers, were John and Harriet Wicker. He was from Scotland, but this Harriet was a local girl. They both worked at the Bryant and May matchbox factory in Fairfield Road, Old Ford, Bow.

The factory was a large and imposing place, like the tenements were. Homes like warehouses; and they were making damp-proof matches, for the troops like us, and this was dangerous work.

Floors and floors of men and women breathed in the poisonous yellow phosphor and sulphur fumes not unlike the poison of the gas bombs we will get 'Gas, gas, quick boys!' and gas mask-up as we had been trained to do here on the Western Front.

Before we were born, The Match Girls as they were known, and everyone knew of them. They, went on strike, stooped work, and people still spoke about it for years afterwards.

The girls refused to work for poor wages and in such deplorable conditions. Do you remember us being told about it? Annie Besant and The London Matchgirls Strike, they called it; because only the women walked out, while the men continued working, and earning wages.

But the products could not be finished without the women. The bosses - the wealthy Bryant and May families - were Quakers and Pacifists, and they had a social conscience. They either had to close the factory or pay fair wages and provide safer working conditions.

Whether what they paid John and Harriet afterward was ever going to be fair, is another question. We, us, our soldiers to pay, anyway. As with war, fairness doesn't really come into it. It is like everyone for themselves, and together with their comrades.

Like here with us, Harry, me and you.

Fairness, and not fairness, I'd say.

The girls refused to work, went on strike, and won. Just like when we strike their matchsticks at the front, now, eh? No second chances. All or nothing! We win. Those workers could have been fired. Like Father was in 1914 from the Morocco Goods Warehouse. 'Let go', they said, 'Laid-off'. No trade was going to travel from Morocco to London now. Only U-boats from the so-called North German Sea into the North Atlantic. Disrupting trade with Africa, the Americas and Canada, and the Far East.

Then, in 1914, there was nowhere else for us to go except back to Sussex, then Croydon, and then Brighton. Safety from the Zeppelins and the German bombing. And now we, too, have to stick it out. Now we are here. Strike first, surprise strike. Survive it only if you're lucky, eh? Like being down a shell hole, waiting for the next attack.

"Put that light out!" is all we would get now.

Like the Home Guard at home. Here it is strike once and hope there are not any sharp shooters around hiding in the woods and thickets. Light a tobacco quickly, cupped in hand, and draw. Then keep it away from you, cupped in hand. If you're unlucky, you might only lose a hand and not your whole bloody head! Unless they were such bad shots, eh?

You never know, especially in the dark. Not so bad if you lose a finger and spend the rest of the war in Blighty, eh?

Of course, we all thought ourselves invincible.

It couldn't happen to us, until it did. Then there really was no going back.

There were times when I almost wished one of those cigarettes might be the last, if only just to end the suspense. I might just think to myself, *Well, if this is going to be the last one, so be it!* I don't know so much now. Anymore. One way or another.

Maybe better to die out here, than to live a coward's life? Or worse. Fatal injury may be better than any other. I don't mind, so just get on with it. Let's win, and get this thing over with! So we do get on with it, don't we?

We cannot strike now, can we? Even matches. Silent marching. No songs or stories, no birdsong. We cannot refuse to fight now. Not once we're here, getting shot at. Not now we are both here, at the Western Front, France, eh?

Chapter 8: Alfred Byfield

Alf could have enlisted, but he said if he had children, if he had boys of fighting age, he would not let them go, and he would not go either. Alfred Byfield is Mother's brother-in-law by Aunt Etty, our cousin Henrietta.

He was against the war, any war. He would have been the age for enlisting or conscription. He was a self-employed glazier and younger than our father, who did enlist voluntarily even before conscription.

Uncle Alf did not have children then, and he did not agree with the war. By the start of the Great War in 1914, he had married Etty, and Cousin Gracie had married Uncle Walter, my only familiar namesake. Walter was opposed to the Great War as well. This Walter Southgate had been brought up in Hackney Road, and learned to read and write.

He was trained from the workhouse there in the art of making quill pens, for the Stock Exchange and banks in London. As well as being then a Trades Union clerk, and organiser, he continued making quill pens his whole life.

Serving the City, as I did in some way when I became a messenger at Barclays Bank in Lombard Street in 1914. A short-lived employment, evacuated with Mother to the south coast, as the Zeppelin strikes on London began, and with you and father now abroad.

Uncle Alf. said the war was Imperialistic and all about money. All about the expansion of empires and rivalry in Africa, and although it was fought out in Europe with workingmen's blood.

Uncle Walter said workingmen would never be the winners. Instead, we fought the battles of the Royal Families and Generals who directed operations from afar.

Walter Southgate joined the No-Conscription Fellowship, a group allied with the new Socialist Labour Party and the Suffragette Movement, a campaign to earn women the right to vote.

Walter went to the conscription tribunal, and was found employment on a tomato farm in Kent, which made him an essential worker, and therefore exempt from duty in the war.

The farmhands and labourers would mock and chide him, for being a faint-heart and a coward, and yes, a traitor. He received short shrift and anger from others, once the war had started up. Some of his fellow workers even shut him out of the air raid shelter when the raids started. That soon changed, when those "Conshie" ("conscientious objector") haters were themselves called up in the conscription, to replace the already million dead in the first Somme battle, in 1916.

The farmhands quickly made a pact with the landowner and farmers, to put their names down also as essential workers.

As a result Walter Southgate was sent away, as the work was being done by these *other* 'cowards and traitors' which they were, not. Now far from, and Walter and the other 'Conshies' were no longer needed. Walter continued as an itinerant agricultural labourer in the Hertfordshire and Wiltshire Market Gardens. Like the itinerant agricultural labourer of Father's family a hundred years before.

Walter Southgate worked "feeding the people, not the war," he said. Great Uncle Alf. Byfield, also went to the conscription tribunal, and went as a non-combatant medical auxiliary. To be a stretcher-bearer, on the front line in France.

We may even bump into him there.

There were plenty of those auxiliaries, stretcher-bearers, and nurses back home who'd never thought she would be nursing soldiers from the war, as she did us. Until we were grown to make our own decisions.

They were needed, all of them, these auxiliaries.

Saving lives. Carrying and collecting the wounded and dead is as risky as the fighting. The stretcher-bearers are for the most part unarmed, but are as likely to get sniper shot or bombed as any of us out here. As mother was, nursing back in Brighton, now.

So, Alf. Byfield and Walter Southgate, were against the war. Even though we were told we were going to be invaded if we did not fight and stop the Germans. France and Belgium had already been invaded by the Bosch, and we were next if we did not take the fight to them. Even into North Africa, Egypt, and French-Morocco, as Father had told us. We had to crush the Hun, we were told, or they would end the Empire.

And us? What would we do about it?

I don't know if we would have been invaded if we didn't fight, or if we'd have lost the empire. I have no idea what state the world would be in if the Great War had not happened. Then again, neither does anyone else.

We could not take any chances, could we? We could be against the war, but that doesn't matter now. It has started without us having any say at all, so it seems. No vote.

But isn't that always the way in wars? Chickens don't vote for Xmas! Or the Conscription Bill.

Reducing the sign-up age, for training, battle ready, ready for the front. It's all the same. It may not have made any difference to us in the end, if we had been invaded, or if we had sued for peace, if that was possible. The Germans were after The Empire; and we were Home, and Colonial, after all.

Indian, Ghurkha, Australian and American and Canadian, African and Caribbean and everyone else out here from our WorldWide Empire. It was the rich and ruling classes in London and the shires, and the aristocratic lords and ladies, who had capitalist shopping streets, and socialist housing estates, named after themselves.

They were at risk of losing their wealth, as well as all of ours! All our families were related somehow to this wealth, but only at the distance they remain from us now. The politicians and generals and royalty remain at home, and in the back camps, far from the front.

For each of us fighting at the front line, whether off the land, or offices or shopworkers, the debate was totally inconsequential. Many tens of thousands resisted, and refused to fight. Either exempted, or escaped. They, avoided the conscription, one way or another. But, like now the already killed, they were not counted, or talked about, anymore, inside the family or out.

The rest of us, perhaps, did not have the guts to stand up against it, or to run and hide; or to face the tribunal. Go to prison, or to carry stretchers, or simply to grow food for the people.

There was a lot of encouragement to join up, to put it mildly. There was the need for paid work.

We were entreated by God, King, and Country; and by popular entertainers from the music halls and cinema, who would perform for the public and troops at home, and abroad, some of them.

But few of these would actually end up fighting.

Some would, and some – many - would die in the fighting as well. Many writers and poets and artists.

Many families decided among themselves who would stay

behind and who would go. One way or another, they found their various ways. Most of us who went to war may have had little to lose for ourselves but for our family to continue; and thus, we had everything to gain.

Our own father Mark Mepham, had reasonable cause to go in our places. Maybe it would all be over by Xmas, or before I would be old enough to fight.

We - You and I Harry, in the indestructible moments of youth—we went anyway.

And so here am I in a field in France. Now you have heard of the Kentish and Sussex Mephams and the London Coultehurst-Wells.

A Frenchman from the trenches told me the Wells name in French is "Dupuis" meaning "by the well," just as "Dupres" means "by the field," or Byfield.

In France and in Belgium, and German, even. We might yet have distant cousins by blood or marriage. From Roman, Norman, Anglo-Saxon, or more recent Georgian. German times, people with whom we are fighting with, or against. The German Mephams still, of some ancient King Meapha.

For what? To kill or be killed—the same.

Part Three: Sarajevo

Chapter 9: The Assassination in Sarajevo 1914.

The assassination in Sarajevo was all over the newspapers.

Franz Ferdinand, Archduke of Austria-Hungary, was

assassinated by a lone student in Sarajevo, Serbia, June 1914. He -

they - royals were expendable, an excuse for starting a war, so it

seemed. Austria sent an ultimatum to Serbia, bringing in for some

reason, the Russians and French, and new German nationhood. The

headlines on the newspapers read:

ASSASSINATION IN SARAJEVO!

CRISIS IN THE BALKANS! CRISIS IN EUROPE!

WAR IS DECLARED!

In July, tsarist Russia mobilized against Austria-Hungary in

support of Serbia. Germany declared war on Russia. In August 1914,

France—bound by treaty for mutual protection with Russia—was

invaded by German troops via Flanders. France immediately

withdrew its troops six miles from the German border onto the

ridges of Alsace-Lorraine and along the plains, ahead of the German-held railway junction at Cambrai.

The German Armies, after the initial unprovoked invasion against Belgian (whose cruel and deranged ruler was another member of the European aristocracy), the Central Armies continued to threaten northward toward the then-North German Sea, the English Channel, and on to Paris itself.

London would be next, we were told.

The German Kaiser, Wilhelm, dynastic cousin of the British King and Russian Tsar, pleaded, apparently, with his Generals to pull the German troops back from France and Belgium. The German chief of staff, Von Moltke, veteran from the Franco-Prussian war, had unfinished business and ignored his Kaiser. The British allies of France, Belgium, and Russia, declared war on Germany and the Central powers, on 4th August 1914.

Winston Churchill, of the aristocratic Marlborough family, was First Lord of the Admiralty. He was also the head of the British Committee of Imperial Defence. Based on friendly trade relations with France in Africa, and determined antagonism toward Germany, this committee had started making war plans in advance of 1914.

Under the initial command to block the way to Paris from

Brussels, as at the battle of Waterloo one hundred years previously. But, with different sides, and the fact that the German Army had passed Brussels, and Waterloo, and reached the Somme river, in France.

The British Expeditionary Forces immediately became entrenched across great swathes of land in Belgium and France, and began to push the Germans back, with some success. Back to the Somme river, Mons, Ypres, and the Hindenburgh-Siegfried line at Cambrai.

In 1915, following the disastrous Italian Greek Gallipoli Turkey campaign, Syria and Russia, and the then Ottoman Mughal Empire, and the revolutionary General Ataturk. With the Aussies and Anzac Brigades many lost, which our father Mark did survive.

We knew only by brief letter delivered, that Mark Henry, was in Egypt.

Churchill was stood down. Churchill, who had fought the Boer in south Africa in that war of 1902, commanded briefly the Sixth Battalion Royal Scots Fusiliers, with General Haig, at the new Western Front, in France. Before returning to the London government, as Secretary of State for War and Munitions.

As a personal friend of Churchill, Conan Doyle advised and recommended that the crews of military vessels, submarines, and ships should be supplied with lifebelts and lifeboats; and, for the first time front-line soldiers were to wear body armour.

That is why we wear these flak jackets now, as we wait for the orders to advance on Cambrai. Now, I can imagine Grandfather Mark and Grandmother Fanny Mepham buried together at Uckfield, East Sussex.

I can imagine our mother Caroline nursing the injured and wounded in Brighton, from the Western Front. She could have heard the roar of cannon from Flanders fields, in the spring and summer, and into the autumn, at Ypres and Paschendale, and Somme, into the winter of 1917.

I came to France in May 1916.

Harry Arthur, you were returned home after the battles to the north in Ypres and the Somme for rest and recuperation. Mother was at Croydon, then Brighton, nursing the dead and wounded.

You, with the many thousands of others expected the informal winter truce, sparing us bombardment; and then home, to be returned for the expected final push the following year, in 1918.

In 1917, I, Walter Mepham, I fought with the Third Army on the Siegfried-Hindenburg line, and now at Cambrai.

Taking your place, Harry. At the back camps and the battlefields. We are digging new trenches further south, moving closer to those of the German Army, and the Hindenburg Line.

South of your lines at the Somme, Harry. Although we are never to meet again, Harry, I know what you then knew and as mother despairingly knew, already.

That since we met up in Brighton in 1916, that I am not to ever to return home, or to see you, or her, in life, again.

Chapter 10: The Decision Is Made

Prior to 1914, Germany had been stockpiling guns, motorized cannon, mechanized tanks, warships, and aircraft. As Churchill and Conan Doyle had warned they would threaten our empires, with the Austrians and Hungarians, the Ottoman Turks, and eventually across the north Baltic Sea into Eastern Europe with the Russians in Crimea again, and to the Far East, Japan and China.

Eventually, with the colonial and former colonial realms of Australia, the East Indies and the Americas, the Near East and North Africa. Egypt, the Belgian French Congo, and then Morocco; and the European colonies in Africa, where it had all started. The European War, the Great War - a World War they could not have imagined.

Overruling the Kaiser, Hutier and Hindenberg formed the German Supreme Council. The imperialistic military and industrial dictatorships of the new German nation established by the "Nation-Builder" Bismarck were effectively deposed, as was the Kaiser from the seat of power. Germany was once again asserting itself in Europe, wanting to takeover, or be given a share in the adventurous trading colonial world of Britain and France.

It was a glorious summer in London, and at the seaside at Hastings in 1914, you Harry Arthur were just nineteen, and I, Walter, was just seventeen years old, too young to serve, as you and father both did.

By then, the Morocco Warehouse where Father worked had closed, and there was no work in London. Father had no other city trade, other than that of warehouseman and salesman, and an economic depression loomed, or had already started, with unemployment rising and restrictions on trade.

Many of us, the people we knew and family, believed the economic slump was brought on by the greed of those at the top and restricted trade for the rest of us!

The Great Depression of the 1920s, it was later said, was delayed only by the start of the Great War. We were staying back in Catsfield, near Battle, Hastings. Father and you, Harry Arthur, both out of work, signed-up for the war, 1914, at Ore in Sussex. We never really discussed if any of us would or should sign up. Father must have been too old at fifty-four years if Conan Doyle was at forty-four, but he signed up anyway.

Father must have had something special to offer, although what a miller's labourer, grocer's and draper's assistant, warehouseman, and salesman had to offer exactly, I could not tell. Unless it was some knowledge and experience of Morocco and North Africa for which he yearned. Perhaps the running of the army stores like a country shop.

Father did see action throughout and latterly back here at the Western Front, too. The last of his days, as he never returned home, as I did not either. To see you, or our Mother again.

But we knew he wanted to go and died to no avail, of this, from his first ever journey overseas, he was never to return.

He may have lied about his age - many did that - perhaps to fight instead of you and me, Harry Arthur, and he was accepted as you were. Once recruited and trained, all of us at Aldershot, Hampshire.

Father was never questioned further. Father joined the Royal Sussex Regiment as Private TF201401, Fourth Battalion. He trained at Horsham, went to Egypt and Suvla Bay, Gallipoli. In August 1915, aged fifty years.

You, Harry Arthur, joined the Royal Fusiliers, Ninth

Battalion, and went to Aldershot, mobbed from Croydon to Crowborough Camp, Sussex, and landed in France in 1915.

The Army would not take me to start with, and Mother and Father seemed relieved. It would not last long, they said, this war, and I would do a better job at home in a trade that protected me from enlistment, even as an agricultural labourer. Unlike our father and his parents and their parents before them, I had never done agricultural work in my life, apart from the casual hop-picking. I'd never held a gun, either, or fought a battle except with you and our cousins, hops, and small stones, which were dangerous enough.

At first, not enough men signed up to fight. Why would they? Why wouldn't they?

This reluctance or willingness was perceived rational self-interest, according to Russell, or 'work with pay' in anyone else's terms. It had nothing to do with National Pride or Socialism at home, or Communism in Russia. It had nothing to do with duty under God and King, according to others. Although either of these would have been perhaps the more rational, as spiritual, reasons to fight, or not to fight. There was a weighted choice, and a decision to be made, as well as livelihood, and family.

The government said they had to meet force with force, and did not have enough troops to confront the Kaiser's army. They introduced the Conscription Acts in 1916.

As Uncle Arthur said at the time, it was like being in a firing squad, with a gun aimed at your head too. Who would fire first? Neither, or both.

Uncle Alf said he would shoot the bastards first. Whom he meant was unclear—those who avoided conscription, or the enemy?

In 1916, The Conscription Act of Parliament called on all able-bodied men without dependants, nineteen to forty years old, to join up. At the end of the war, there is an unwritten promise of pension paid to the family, should we die, or be unable to work, with unemployment benefits. The alternative to conscription, is imprisonment.

Word spread quickly that some deserters had already been shot by firing squad in France. Whether this was true, we did not know, but it had an effect. We did know then what we know now. That they were "shell shocked" as we start to say out here, with fear, and had turned their backs on the battlefield and refused to fight anymore.

As you did, Harry, as you did.

As their individual sense of reason told them to do: for themselves and for their families. An irrational, or rational action, in whose rationality?

But they could not go on, whatever the threat to themselves.

Would that have made a difference to our already made up decisions? If we had not known that? That I would be killed anyway. As you, Harry, as Mother must have. As I have come to know? As everyone at this Front; at this point in time and place, knows is possible, even likely.

As you told mother on that final leave of duty: as some said' The hell that is war but for some heaven of winning.'

We did believe the propaganda and threats, most of us, whether death by firing squad or invasion. Whether it would really happen like that or not, we would take no chances. I was only sixteen years old, anyway, by the time of conscription, and I lied, as Father did, and I enlisted. No questions asked.

We had moved again, Mother and I, to another rented place in Croydon, South London, 28 Boswell Road. It was near to the hospital where Mother was a nurse administering to the troops who made it back, patching them up physically, at best, to be returned to the front, which not many did, or were able to.

You, Harry, stayed with us that one time, when you were home on leave from the Western Front, Harry. You had been at the first Ypres battle in Belgium, but didn't tell us much about it. Returned again, to make up the numbers from the millions killed in the first Battle of The Somme.

You, in time for the second, 1916, the same, as bloody and deadly. Mother knew anyway, and told me. About the fatally injured, she saw, and nursed, who did return home.

Only then few survived. They were brought the hospital to Brighton because they were dying on their way to south London, Croydon, and mother moved there.

I could not say I did not know for what I was signing up. And when you survived the second, then at The Somme again, and were home. We talked about most things growing up in Paddington. Then when we moved to St. Giles in East London, and we carried on our ways.

We were all back in Hastings, with the Mepham family, by the start of the war, 1914.

Then, when Father, and you had left, for the last time. Mother and I moved back to the outskirts of South London, to Thornton Heath, Croydon, Surrey.

For her nursing, for me waiting to leave for the Western Front that we could hear from across The British Channel. Now, the North Sea and Baltic and Atlantic fought over and under, and by land and air. In London. Where the Germans dropped their first RFA 501 zeppelin incendiary bomb in 1915 through 1916. The hospital was hit would you believe it?

This was called the 'Theatre-Land Raid' in the newspaper headlines. The bombs fell on Piccadilly Circus and Shaftsbury Avenue, and Oxford Street. We knew about the deaths and injuries of civilians and workers, essential workers, fire-fighters. I could have done that work instead. But I did not.

I wanted to get them back. Using the River Thames for guidance, the Zeppelins bombed factories on the river Lea. Then dumped the remainder on the south, before they fled back to Germany.

When we were all away at the war, then Mother moved back down to Brighton, Sussex. To nurse the returning wounded there.

The soldiers were dying on their way to Croydon from Brighton, she said, and she would be nearer to us, across the English Channel.

Despite what you said to Mother, and Mother said to me, then, when I was old enough to enlist, for training only, until I was nineteen years, they said, and I signed the form.

I joined the London and Scottish regiment, Twenty-Sixth Battalion, 12685, registered private in the Royal Fusiliers Ninth 23792, signed up at Woolwich, London, and was taken out to Hounslow, then Aldershot, for training.

I could not be sent abroad until I was nineteen anyway, so they said. I trained enthusiastically, my theatre of war then being then at Aldershot, Hampshire, as described on my papers.

After only a few weeks' training—learning offensive actions, attacking straw bags with bayonet and wooden club, digging and trenching, and so on—we were taken by train from Aldershot to Paddington station, then on to Waterloo station and the South Coast.

From Aldershot to Paddington station, then along Oxford Street nearby where we used to live by Bloomsbury.

Still busy in the daytime, another newsboy calling out the news from the newsstand at the corner of New Oxford Street. There were few people in and out of the remaining small shops and the large department stores.

Everything was quite normal except the Streets of London were empty; and the windows of buildings broken from the air blasts, boarded and blacked-out.

The banks and trading offices ceased, almost emptied, once the City Clerks Battalions and Pals and Chums together, if they all get killed. A whole generation of men, and women and children seeing all this. The Battalions had so enthusiastically been started in 1914. I was relieved anyway from my short-lived work at the post room at Barclays Bank, in London. I was too young then to go to war, and went with you, Harry Arthur, and Mother and Father back to Sussex.

It never occurred to me, even then, that I might never see Sussex, or those London streets and buildings, so familiar to our growing up, ever again.

This time, I, went on the Army commissioned tram through empty streets—empty of once enthusiastic crowds. Some few of them kept up the façade of hope and shouted good wishes.

Others, no doubt, glad it was not themselves or their brothers or sons going to war. But by now no one could dissent in public for fear of white feathering, or arrest. Words and plucked feathers were thrown like stray bullets, insults of treachery, cowardice, and laggardness, and, no doubt, worse. Russell was imprisoned.

Conan Doyle was in France reporting for the War Office and newspapers.

As we went over Waterloo Bridge, there was no cheering into the station, and it was no longer festooned with banners and flags. We were then taken directly and away to France. No stopping off at cosy Crowborough Camp for us.

By overcrowded paddle steamer we were ferried over the Channel to Havre, and onward south by crowded train, like cattle herded. Marching on foot to set up camp behind the front line, our only orders — Stay Put and Be Ready! I was nineteen years old, and six months when we moved into battle formation, facing distantly the church spires we would see, and the Ridge, overlooking Cambrai.

Chapter 11: France

Behind the lines in France, we are far enough away from the fighting to imagine there is no war going on and everything is normal as it was at home, except for the shortage of eligible bachelors, like you and me eh?! Here, we are nightly going forward, digging in and reinforcing supplies, communication and reserve trenches.

Navvy work really. Construction Pioneers we are called, sometimes. Navvies under cover of night, soldiers by day. We returned to the safety of valley villages. The French played cards, sang songs, drank beer and wine, and we all had plentiful rations.

Over the fields and hills to the north and east, bangs and explosions split the air often for days at a time. I think of you, Mother, and Father frequently Harry Arthur, wondering whether you were thinking of us.

Mother may have been able to hear the rackety noise of warfare back in Sussex, and even in London, sending all the birds out of the trees into the sky and away from the threat.

Few of the troops passing through return this way. They go

straight to the front, and the very few we see again are dead, or severely injured and soon transported back to hospital in Blighty.

They experienced the horror of Ypres and the Somme river valley but like you Harry, they do not speak of it.

Here. Others limp back from Passchendaele, infantry and dismounted cavalry, while their rider-less, and unsaddled horses gallop as far away as possible, fear in their snorting heads.

They crash wildly into ditches and collide with trees, disappearing who knows where. Some were butchered, we were told, for army food.

Light aircraft occasionally fly over, photographing our positions and strafing us with almost harmless machine guns. Otherwise we live a quiet country life with the cavalry horses in the fields and the local French girls and their families continuing their lives as if little had changed.

But they still live in fear and subdued hatred as we do. Their loved ones are often lost; in fact, I don't think I remember any French soldiers returning, injured or otherwise. There were some deserters, refusers in hiding, we were told, and others with French Marshal Foch to the south of us here.

We dig trenches at night, and not by the full moon, so we can take cover as soon as we hear the enemy spotter planes overhead. In the daytime they are sometimes shot down by our hidden anti-aircraft fire, before they can return radio messages.

But the German ground bombardments draw nearer and become more intense from the northeast it seems, often continuing all day and lasting for days on end; and it is as if the war is being lost. We stay put. Even though we are anxious and want to go in, it is as if we are being saved for something special, we in the infantry—the poor bloody infantry—we are always the last to get the command. No time to think about it, just get on with it.

We help retrieve and re-saddle the riderless horses that somehow find their way back to the camps, but we are never allowed to ride them across the fields and farms.

The horses have a wild and terrified look in their eyes, as do the troops returning on foot. They become fewer and fewer as the days pass. We pass our time with the sworded dragoons, the lancers, and hussars, and an Indian regiment of cavalry who know horses as we, most of us, do not.

These dark-skinned soldiers, some with turbans over their

helmets, laugh and chat in a strange language of their own. Their English strongly accented.

Some Chinese are here as well, digging trenches with us. That's how we know it is an Imperial Empire Colonial war and a world war, all right. Some of the Indians wear full beards and long hair in turbans, which they aren't allowed to trim for religious reasons, we discovered.

The China were fighting the Japanese, in the East, who declared war on Germany and China and sunk the German Fleets in the Pacific and South China Seas.

I, however, do manage to shave.

For me, once a week is all that was needed. I was then, since March 14th 1917, just nineteen years and six months old.

Chapter 12: Reports of War

We knew the great Conan Doyle, of course. He was here at Cambrai to send reports to the newspapers, magazines, and also the war office. Most of us knew the early serialisations of the *Challenger* stories and the *Sherlock Holmes* mysteries from rough paperback books sold in bookshops, and at street corner stalls.

The resemblance to Suffolk and the chalky South Downs here *is* remarkable, and we feel a strange connection to our homeland across the English Channel. Occasionally, during this long last march, we encounter lookout posts behind. Some with tents and huts, tables and chairs set out.

On them sit the Generals and Field-Marshals, and once, we were told, just before we were called to order and set to moving up, there sat Sir Arthur Conan Doyle.

Conan Doyle was visiting as a medical officer, and reported on "The Great War". He was on the line between Villecourt to the north and Villers Ghislaine to the south. At the strategic high ground at Bourlon at "the important town of Cambrai," he wrote described the Western Front as made up "of trenches and cannon at the Siegfried Line so-called of the German Hindenburg Line."

Conan Doyle wrote in admiration of the "impressive fortifications "a Cyclopean work...Huge and solid a modern monument, and a wonder of the world...enormous excavations of prodigious length, depth, and finish...object lessons both of the strength of the Germans, the skill of their engineers, and the ruthlessness with which they exploited the slave and captive labour with which so much of it was built."

In the summer of 1917, British General Plumer had taken the Messines Ridge at Flanders to the north of the Siegfried Line, with an initial heavy bombardment of artillery, then with Lewis machine guns. With rifle grenades and skirmishing infantry groups. Plumer had the express but unrealised strategic aim of reaching, attacking, and destroying the German U-boat submarine fleet in the Belgian ports, and so headed north rather than south to Cambrai.

As Conan Doyle had predicted, the German fleet had been harassing British supplies in the English Channel and North Sea. Conan Doyle's reports from the Western Front, however, now reported "severe losses and no ground gained, and no advance on the coast…attacks from further tank and infantry attacks at Ypres, Somme, and most recently at Paschendale.

The Germans had withdrawn to their Hindenburg line Arras to Rheims arched west just four miles in front of Cambrai, facing the British and Allied lines." Cambrai was taken by the Germans in the first invasion in 1914.

The Cathedral city was a significant German supply railhead, and rest and recreation point for their early successes, won by the rapidly deployed trench warfare along the hundreds of miles of the Western Front. Strategically significant in blocking any newly attempted advance toward Paris, the City of Cambrai was now also a diversion from the stalled aim of stopping a northward and the coastal German advance northward through Luxembourg, Belgium, and Holland.

The French were all but defeated in the south. With many of their tanks destroyed at Arras and their armies slaughtered from the German high ground along the Alsace line, for the iron and coal mines, the French troops deserted, went into hiding early on, and some of them openly mutinied.

Those many that remained now joined with the British and commonwealth allies under Marshal Foch. The Canadians, Anzacs, Chinese, Indians, and Americans were now arriving. All of us drawn up in camps and trench lines. The Allies were now holding the north up to the coast, while the French continued to fight the Germans for the coal and iron ore fields of Alsace-Lorraine to the south.

The Russians fought the Germans in the east, extending the Eastern Front to the Turkish Ottoman Empire, also drawn into the conflict early on. Neither side on either front was able to outflank the other. Soldiers faced each other with increasing ferocity on all fronts, lost in the clouds of flamethrowers, artillery and machine gun barrage, poison gas, mines, and grenades.

Our aircraft support glided over the increasingly vast area of concrete shelters and underground works at the Siegfried Line.

We had "ineffectual counter battery artillery fire," according to Conan Doyle, Conan Doyle however praised Field Marshal Haig taking over from Churchill as chief of the command and his "brain and his daring planning at the assault on the Hindenburg Line at Cambrai," and "for his determination to strike the first blow, without prior bombardment warning."

Hidden, camouflaged tank regiments were now to lead the surprise attack at Cambrai with air support, for the cavalry and infantry following on.

As the summer of 1917 came to a close, the weather conditions worsened. It was apparently a widespread belief among the general staff that there were sufficient infantry remaining and assembled "with some of the most seasoned fighting material in the army battered, but fighting fit, to take advantage of a surprise attack toward Cambrai," according to Conan Doyle.

In early November, we were moved up from Peronne, toward Cambrai, south of the devastated Somme battlefield. Leading up through Flanders to the coast, the ground was burned and blown to smithereens, the Somme river below as dark as the muddy fields. Mud was all around, and we were dug in all along the line from Soissons to Rheims.

Our division was one of the newly recruited Kitchener armies. K1 conglomerated, along with remains of other depleted regiments, merged into the massive Third Army, which in the end included Canadians, South Africans, Indian, Chinese, Scots, Welsh, English, and Irish all mixed and merged to make up the numbers. A thousand men went into each battalion with five companies of two hundred each under thirty officers.

Sergeants and a sergeant major, then the corporals, lieutenants, leading captains-major remained behind with the Generals and general-staff on the high back hills watching as we marched ahead.

Each of us privates was under a non-commissioned officer platoon group with four platoons to a company. There were signals on bicycles, and drivers of horse-drawn vehicles, pack horses, and draught horses pulling the armoury and ammunition carts. As well as the water carts, rations carts, tool carts with shovels, hand axes, pickaxe, spares, and other parts for the gunnery, and for the brigade of machine gunners drawn up ahead, ready to be armed and fired into action.

Horses hooves and wheels broke up the sunken roads and high fields as we crossed. We marched at night, in single line, along the wooden planked and boarded corduroy roads, toward the new front. Bicycles ferrying messages and accounts to the rear trenches as we went.

Rifles and bayonets were handed out and prepared. Medics

and stretcher-bearers, the drummers and band musicians walked silently behind.

We marched at ease at night. No talking, no smoking.

We were to rendezvous at Fins at three o'clock in the morning of 20 November 1917, just getting light, ready for six o'clock signals.

The French troops moved south.

We freshly of the infantry were brought up from the farmlands. The sun just started to rise in the cloudy sky. With the newly allied and colonial troops, we remained at dawn awaiting orders. Section leaders had colour charts indicating streamer and light signals to be made out on maps.

It was like a great game with us as pieces, set out as on a board. We infantrymen—we did not know anything of what was going to happen. We were always last to be told. It was overcast with weather conditions worsening. It had been steadily raining and despite the conditions, the sun only just appearing through the clouds. As if lightning and thunder let loose, the attack was launched at dawn.

Chapter 13: The Cambrai Operation

The Cambrai Operation, the Third Army under General Byng, Phase One: A ten-kilometre front consisting of tanks and a thousand heavy artillery guns with fourteen squadrons of the Royal Flying Corps standing by; and two divisions of horse cavalry to break through the enemy lines, followed by the six divisions of infantry.

Lieutenant Colonel Fuller of the British Tank Corps had recommended attacking with tanks in the dry, wide plain between the St. Quentin Canal and the Canal du Nord. This would take them over chalk soil rather than over snarling marshes and heavy muddy clay.

This recommendation was taken up by the Third Army Commander Byng, the commander on the ground, and then vetoed by Commander-in-Chief Haig who had taken overall command in 1916 (replacing the British General French, who was sent to quell the Irish Republican Army Easter Uprising in Dublin).

Generals Haig and Kitchener wanted a quick victory to finish off the year of defeats. Haig, as Conan Doyle noted, changing his former praise to scorn, "disingenuously ordered a surprise tank attack on the Germans at the Hindenburg Line and eventually at the town of Cambrai."

Byng then changed the plan to destroy enemy positions with tanks and withdraw. In order to make a breakthrough on the German lines, he ordered the cavalry and infantry to the front to follow the tank attack.

This, "for the last assault before the winter," the surprise attack "necessitated the absence of preliminary bombardment," as was otherwise usual with attacks against enemy positions "as this would have been a pre-warning of the infantry assault to come."

The orders to move up were given, horses were harnessed, and the cavalry saddled up, riding the line around and ahead. Overhead, light aircraft buzzed among shouts of command, and the order was carried out. As we moved ahead, tanks prepared weeks in advance, camouflaged and hidden, were appearing from buildings and wooded undergrowth. In lines, they moved forward in the hundreds, the cavalry now flanking, and we the infantry following on.

This was to be a massed tank attack successful, it had been

said, at the Somme; and we now "crawling toward the trysting-place, with the colossus," Conan Doyle wrote, "as if some new yet ancient legend or tragedy with a yet recent unity of time and place were being played out."

General Ellis in the forward tank fired the shot, and the whole lot went off.

The cavalry followed around, and we of the foot infantry followed in ranks behind the tanks. Falling-in, as instructed, behind our colour-coded marker tank just after dawn. The ditches ahead leapt by the horse cavalry, and we followed on traversing over cut trench wires, posts crashing down, and burning bundles of wood fascines flamed fearsomely as grapnel tanks tore aside the heavily barbed wire, rolling forward, crossing and occasionally crashing into the gaping ditches.

A smoke barrage hid just about everything. The numbered marks on the rear of the tank we attempted to follow could hardly be made out. The tanks lead, firing ahead all the time, blazing across trenches as remaining German troops fired on, and on fire surrendering even as they died. The motorized tanks drove straight through, over the charcoaled, burning remains of bodies.

We followed on in a single line many miles long, silent with fixed bayonets. The cavalry moved through the breaches, the tanks rolled on, ever advancing. The smoke choked us, and the horses were utterly terrified. The tanks were reinforced steel, but looked flimsy despite their size, great tractor wheels, and guns pointing forward.

It was the first time I had seen these tanks from the infantry lines and they did look as Conan Doyle described, "like a herd of gray African elephants charging ahead, blowing dust from the fields, as the chalk dried in the wind." Below, a whole field lay out, muddier toward the centre where trenches lay like water-filled irrigation moats.

Concrete bunkers set out the connecting points between miles and miles of undercrossed main and support lines, "Deep, the size of a three-story house, and reinforced like an underground city…" this was Conan Doyle's "…colossus: The Siegfried Line". Missiles flew ahead from the tank's gun turrets. The gunners shouted down instructions to the unsighted driver as mud splattered into the quagmire below foot.

We cheered as German bodies flew into the air, the smoke cast a pall over the early morning and created its own deathly haze.

A tank crashed into a water-filled trench, un-retrieved dead, it's and their war, over.

Some of the tanks were hit by the German forward gun batteries which were concealed behind the remaining walls of deserted villages and farms. As we trudged on in the mud and rain, many of the tanks careened to a halt, stuck in the mud and ditches, guns pointing at ugly angles. Some were hit by artillery fire, shattered with all inside.

Those Germans surprised by the sudden dawn appearance fled at first sighting, were killed or taken prisoner, or had fallen back to let their overhead artillery assaults freely devastate our ranks.

We took prisoners. We disarmed them and sent them through to the back lines; and we were to continue now in pursuit of the others fleeing. The tanks and infantry had done their work, and not a sound hardly from the Hun now. Their dead and injured were allowed to be carried off, while the remainder retreated to the wooded tops of the next hills.

At several hundred yards distance, we were ordered to hold

our positions in and around the deserted and shattered village of Havrincourt.

Thankful to be alive, we hunkered down for the night.

Eight thousand prisoners were taken on that first day, and sent back through the lines, lucky beggars, and a hundred gun positions were also taken out.

The sun rose late the next day. It was autumn anyway, but the foggy thick pall of smog lay everywhere, moving up with an eastward breeze, not yet settled into the day. Once in clear, frosty, autumn midday sunshine, we were moved up toward Flesquieres.

As the air cleared in the breeze, it felt like a walk in the country. Hardly anything stirred. The sound of birdsong filled the quietness. In midmorning, the warring sides waited during the informally agreed breakfast truce. We were accustomed to this well-established routine used to recoup and recover before stating our deadly intentions.

On this day, the human combatants were as an assuming army of reoccupation. The songbirds were soon distant, and on silent desertion from the scene.

This was not the most joyous of days. The marching songs

were not sung, and we stayed alert, awaiting the first firing shot, commencing the day's work.

The Germans had retreated and were nowhere to be seen. Even on the hills, they had retreated further than the day before. But our progress was slow, now in the salient land marked out on the maps, culminating at Cambrai.

The tanks and the cavalry were held up by the canals and the mud, but we of the infantry marched on alone and without cover. Through the devastated landscape, we trudged southwest in the tracks of the retreated Germans, and our own stalled tank attack.

Along the canals and roads, through villages and ruined hamlets, toward Marcoing. The bridges had been blown up at our advance and completely destroyed. Little was left anywhere, but for great holes in the ground, and battered walls half-standing owing to our artillery the previous day, or so it seemed.

Making the trek more treacherous. But, at least giving cover at times, even if it was up to your ankles or knees in muddy, dirty water. Sometimes bloated bodies floated in the water. We came under constant and unpredictable barrage from well-hidden Germans, with superior machine guns.

Still, we trudged past the blasted village and canals, across open country utterly changed with the ruts of squadrons and brigades marching across. With the cavalry on horseback, and the last few tanks remaining, the canals could not be crossed.

The Royal Engineers were hampered with their makeshift bridges. We encountered obstacles all along the way. Where the ground had been cleared even of bodies for miles, there were the burning stumps of trees and water wells deliberately blown-up.

Wires and cables lay destroyed amongst the rubble, across the meadows and fields ploughed in, not for the harvest, but so as no cannon or tank could cross.

The villagers had long gone, north and south, to Noyen and Roye, since the first days of the war. Carrying everything they had: clothes, furniture, sewing machines, ovens, chairs and tables, doors and window frames.

Nothing remained before their homes were summarily destroyed by the Germans. Blown to nothing but rubble for the building of the defences at the Siegfried-Hindenburg Line. Most Frenchmen and some women of serviceable age had signed up and gone with the beaten French armies in 1914. While some had deserted and were on the run, many had been taken prisoner and put to work by the Germans building the fortification.

The sites are eerie now, ghostly with their departures and the leaving of so many now dead. Without support, we trudged across open country from bomb crater to bomb crater, not knowing how far the Germans had gone.

The enemy stopped to assault and hold up our advance, with sniper fire and bombardment from the higher ground and woods which were our objective, overlooking the Cambrai plain, and the cathedral City of Cambrai itself.

It was as if they knew who we were, and where we were headed, and had planned their own defence and retreat in advance of our arrival. They had such information now, and so planned, it turned out.

They kept moving back as we moved on along sunken and almost impassable lanes, through villages and hamlets, evacuated and gone, destroyed and deserted. Then, coming into a trap, several explosions ripped the ground and air, and we could not breathe, thrown to the ground.

But we stood again, and kept on walking, following orders

and commands as we went. The population of this area had been moved long before. The buildings were blown-up and completely destroyed by the Germans.

And, as our mortars were being fired, our gunners thought they were hitting German targets, but instead they were reducing the ground to more scorched earth, in the dust and almost impassable mud through which we now trudged.

Keeping up the appearance of trench warfare, snipers and mortars, the German aircraft now flew over, trapping us and bombarding road and train supply lines ahead and behind us. Whiz-bangs shrieked; gas bombs fired, sounding like duds. When the windlass showed the yellow wind was blowing north-easterly, we masked up, or got out of it quick, out of our shell holes to opening fire.

We moved over miles of trenches, a morass of shell holes, bombarded by further heavy mortar from both sides, field gun and machine gun fire, and poison gas. The slow-moving tanks were gradually being taken out, exploded, hit and the crew abandoned, to the muddy trudge of the rest of us, or returned to the back camps.

We headed northeast now, along the canals, passing the

wrecked tanks along lanes circling the woods and copse. We came out into a field that turned out to be the lower reaches of a quagmire through which we had to wade.

We continued onto the dry, chalky slope of another hill, and toward another bombed-out village, where we were stopped and immediately entrenched. On look-out in shifts, we camped for the night. The gunfire calmed down from both sides in an uneasy truce, and we slept uneasily into the next day.

Chapter 14: At Flesquieres

The tank attack had lasted a full two days, 20–21 November 1917. The three-trench system of the Siegfried Line had been pierced for the first time in the war. The German Second Army under Marwitz had retreated, first to Flesquieres, and then to the hilly woodland beyond.

The next morning, the Allied armies covered the miles from Hermies in the north to Gonneleui in the south with the centre of the attack now on the long approach to Flesquieres.

A tangle of heavy gauge wires surrounded the village, set with gun batteries firing molten lead flame. The château on the hill, the manor house below, and the village were heavily defended, but eventually destroyed by the Allies along with those Germans, who had been ordered to stay and defend it.

The remaining tanks, in ragged order, about forty of the initial four hundred, drove straight forward again. Shells were going off all over the place. The tanks now bogged down machine gun fire and light ordnance.

The battle was at first victorious, but not apparently. As we spread across and around Flesquieres the firing ceased, and the cavalry charged ahead.

We followed on, shouting and yelling the whole time as we were instructed to do. The tanks stranded at the lower reaches fired in anger, and may even have hit some of us. They were no good down there and soon quieted.

As we huffed and puffed up the hill, bent forward after the horses, the cavalry spread out, charging again toward the wrecked village.

Many fell, swords aloft, useless against the remaining sighted German guns. It was reminiscent of the disastrous charge of the light brigade at the Russian annexed Crimea more than fifty years earlier, in 1856, as described by Tennyson in *The Charge of the Light Brigade*:

> *"Forward, the Light Brigade!"*
> *Was there a man dismay'd?*
> *Not tho' the soldier knew*
> *Someone had blunder'd:*
> *Theirs not to make reply,*
> *Theirs not to reason why,*

Theirs but to do and die:

Into the valley of Death

Rode the six hundred.

Like them, we were lined up around the hill and ridges, we did not really stand a chance.

We followed on, climbing over dead and injured men and horses of both sides. It did not make our job any easier, leaving dead, dying, and injured men and horses. The infantry were called up, and we rushed up the hill with fixed bayonets at the ready, charged and firing. Ahead, we were stopped and stood watching as the sworded cavalry rounded the millpond river moated perimeter of the village.

The Canadian cavalry were led by Lieutenant Strachan who took over command from the fallen squadron leader. He later received the coveted Cross. The cavalry leapt forward, bridging the river at the edge. We pursued the enemy, taking out a single gun battery. They retreated without their horses, which we took to make up for ours lost, but with several prisoners, and dispersed the rest of the German Sixth and Twentieth infantries. From the north, the Scots Highlanders kept up a battle all day.

We of the infantry continued in from the south. The Highlanders secured the village surroundings, and by nightfall. Flesquieres, a small village, like Mepham in Kent I imagined, was taken. I could have imagined the newspaper headlines back home in New Oxford Street, London, and the calling of a newspaper-seller there:

VICTORY AT CAMBRAI!

Chapter 15: The Boulon Woods

Church bells were rung across Britain for the first time during the war, so the newspapers said.

We did not hear them; we were hardly even in sight of Cambrai. The politicians, Generals and Churchmen, and restricted newspaper reports, led us all on.

Both sides called this a victory, despite the many fallen: the men, horses, and tanks of the apparently triumphant leading infantry divisions. We could not overcome the last of the German resistance. They were soon ensconced on the low hills at the Boulon Woods and beyond, toward Cambrai, preventing our advance from reaching its full limits, whatever they were. If anybody did know, we were not going to take Cambrai. The Cathedral spire rose up in clear view on the plain below.

If it were possible of reaching, taking control of, or destroying Cambrai, we would be victorious, as the newspapers and Conan Doyle had prematurely claimed. Afterward, we doubted that there were any clear strategies or objectives. The Generals, Commanders, and other officers, who appeared occasionally, only to hastily withdraw to the rear again, *they* seemed to be making it up as *we* Went along.

The orders remained indecisive.

We received few and sometimes contradictory orders down the ranks. We remained camped outside Flesquieres, and the next day the Highlanders entered the village and discovered it deserted.

It was the same with the strategic Boulon Wood, overlooking Cambrai. For the next few days, there was little sign of the Hun, who had withdrawn from the area, or at least it seemed so.

Most of our tanks had halted with mechanical problems or had been ditched after being hit. Low flying attacks were made by the air corps on the wood beyond, but with little impact. We were dug in around Flesquieres and then Bourlon Wood, as it would turn out, four or five days.

With the remaining North Country troops, we stormed the last line beyond the village, and then held out against the remaining German divisions. Hidden in the Bourlon Wood and thickets beyond with their heavy guns.

The Germans waited, and we were halted. We remained

throughout the third and fourth days, waiting on orders from headquarters, four miles away at Fins.

Things quietened down, where we were.

Along the line, skirmishes continued into the night, until a self-imposed night-time ceasefire on both sides allowed us to regroup and recover some dead and wounded.

Throughout the explosion-filled days and nights, we wondered all the time where the enemy were, and if they might be moving, and where to? Observing enemy movements was all there was to do until someone fired a shot, and it all went off again.

We also wondered where the remains of our platoons were. Whole divisions and battalions had become separated, survivors joining and forming up with others as best they could. The Ninth Battalion London and Scottish Royal Fusiliers I was now with, had stayed more or less intact. Why the London and Scottish? Because they had lost so many. Communications lines had been broken from headquarters' command.

Following loss of radio contact, there was no one enabled to direct operations on the ground.

We saw the Germans withdraw from Bourlon Wood, as they

had withdrawn from Flesquieres, with heavy resistance, back toward their trench lines on the Cambrai plain, and the surrounding high ground.

The now-deserted wood was taken easily by the Highlanders, as they had taken the village previously.

But then they were repeatedly bombarded with lorry guns and artillery from what remained of the roads and villages beyond, and from the air between us and Cambrai.

With no tanks or heavy guns in position to respond, the Scots infantry divisions were sent into the woods by their commanders, and they were destroyed. All we could hear were the explosions and the screams of men bogged down, trapped in the woods. The Germans strafed them from the air, ground bombed, and gassed the poor wretched souls who were gradually and completely annihilated into a deathly silence.

At the village we were without supplies, numbed with fear and bitterly cold, awaiting the delayed commands of the Generals in their tents, back in safety beyond the real war.

We believed we were trenching down now for the winter around the woods, beyond the shattered village, and only just in view of Cambrai.

Snow was in the air.

Each day started dull and dirty rain from an iron sky. No birds appeared from the trees. Communication and supply trenches behind us were strafed, and we were cut-off by the Germans, despite their initial strategic retreat. We fought sporadically for days, beyond the deserted Flesquieres village. But we were held, pinned down by the artillery fire from the plain below and from hills around.

We remained on that escarpment there for several days with hardly any sleep, rations going short, and our communications and supplies at the rear broken off.

For those days, we forgot about food. It was just for the sleep and the rest from tiredness and the war. We rested in collapsed trenches or out on the open ground, in bomb craters and over-looking the plain. Rum or whiskey helped to dull the pain, the hunger, even to lift tiredness off the body to superhuman effect.

We added it to our tea, not to raise spirits now, but against the cold, and the constant and unpredictable firing, artillery barrage, or aerial bombardment. It helped us to sleep when we desperately needed it, but were unable; it calmed the mind and thoughts. And we returned fire.

We would find a gap in the trench, or wall, or among brushwood, and scramble out, climbing over bodies and not stopping for any injured man screaming. Later, we returned, going back for them with a stretcher-bearer, and all was eerily quiet again.

We had blind faith in non-existent orders.

Staying-put with irrational expectation of rescue. Looking for any success, in this developing disaster, far from victory. The medics arrived during the night, carrying off the injured on stretchers to the tented town and hospital we had left behind.

If they even made it, we never knew, nor did we want to know.

We fought on where we were, and waited for any change, and for it all to come to some kind of end. I had a week's growth of beard. My socks were embedded in the mud in my boots. Frosty morning dew and cold November drizzle settled, melting soggy and soaking through our greatcoats and thick scarves, knitted from home, and wrapped around our helmets.

Sometimes greatcoats taken from the dead, to not perish into the ground with them, and to keep the living alive.

In shifts, we hunkered down to gunfire and explosions all night long. Every day we advanced to just short of the tree covering, opening rifle fire on the heavy German artillery hidden beyond, but we were no closer to Cambrai. The German Armies were now under General Ludendorff, effective head of the third supreme command of the so-called Central Powers, who initially had ordered a counterattack at Flesquieres and Bourlon Wood. It had ended in some failure, as the Germans considered withdrawing from the battlefield back to the garrison city of Cambrai.

But Marwitz brought up more troops—twenty divisions—to begin the counterattack from the hills and plain of Cambrai. These divisions were made up of exhausted men from the failed Eastern Front, released by the cessation of action in Russia after the desertion of the Russian troops from the tsar, and the success of the Bolshevik communist revolution.

The Russians refused to fight for their former master, the Tsar Nicolas, anymore. There was no chance or choice for us. These newly arriving troops from the Eastern Front were complemented by refreshed and younger troops brought in by road and railway from Germany.

A counter-offensive was launched by The Central Command of Germany. Using the Hutier method. A surprise attack at several vulnerable points on the enemy line, first in the northwest, then closing in to the centre, as again at Flesquieres.

As retreat was turned to victory over the stranded British and Allied troops without tanks or big artillery guns remaining, or operable, the Germans were revitalized and reinvigorated.

They broke back through at several places along the Siegfried line—impenetrable once, taken, and now retaken. The Allied Guards Divisions were brought forward, supported by sixteen of the remaining serviceable tanks, holding Gouzeaucourt to the north, and moving onto the Gauche Woods to the south, ending German moves on the town of Metz.

The counterattack at Flesquieres and at the Bourlon Wood started in dense fog. It began at seven o'clock in the morning on 30

November 1917 with flamethrowers and aerial bombardment. The Germans were taking specific points along the line. We did not know where they were, or where we were in relation to them, or each other.

By nine o'clock in the morning, we were dug in again, and we came under sudden and renewed attack. Bodies lay still where they had fallen. Some, injured and untended, died where they were. To the left, to the right, ahead, and behind us all was in a mist, a quietness, a gloom out of which more and more German troops appeared.

The lines of the German infantry, re-grouped and re-equipped, came to meet us over the hills and over the ridges. We heard the screams of the rockets cannoning over our heads as aerial bombardment struck the back trenches, destroying supply and communication, and cutting off our retreat.

Suddenly, the bombardment ceased and marching shoulder-to-shoulder in a grey line toward us was the freshly arrived German infantry.

We fell in again, as the back trenches and shell holes filled with rain turned black with blood. Before us now was the opening ranks of German grey infantry.

At each side still more German troops appeared through the early morning mist, fog, and gun barrel smoke. Turning back and around, and back and around again, with the enemy in full cry at us, we fought shoulder-to-shoulder. But there were thousands of them, infiltrating at so many points and all along the way. We could hear only the screams of the injured, the dying, those blown to pieces.

It was the worst. The worst most of us, mainly new recruits, had seen of the war.

Some of us fell, kept falling, as we turned. We trudged blindly back the way we had come the previous four days in utter disarray.

I was now less sure I would not get hit. I knew now, as I knew all along, it could just as well happen to me. We fought hard. All of the gained ground was being taken back. Back across formerly taken trenches, theirs, then ours, and now theirs again. They charged again, with guns blazing and bayonets fixed, and again we fought back.

Falling back all the time, we turned, forcibly retreated. We were defending, moving toward the back trenches, avoiding shell holes all around, full of dirty water.

I may or may not have fired a last time. I don't know what felled me—a bullet, a piece of shrapnel, or the stab of a bayonet—but with the blast of a shell landing nearby, I stumbled, and I fell.

The shock instantly blinded me. I may have screamed. I was utterly winded, gasping for air, only breathing burning gas and then there was nothing but, silence.

As it continued raining, I was crushed with a searing saw-like pain. Then, I was numb to the pain. I had no longer had any fear. I drowned, buried and mired in a muddy grave, not to rise again, until now.

I had freedom now from any fear.

Perhaps a white stone, perhaps a white or red poppy, black with pollen, swollen as with gunpowder; perhaps a yellow ear of corn in a ripened cornfield is growing there now.

In Memoriam

At the Cambrai Memorial, Louverval, the epitaph reads, "To live in the hearts of those we love is not to die." At the memorial: "Remembered with Honour."

The Memorial Arch at Louverval, France where Walter Mepham is commemorated states, "To God…and to the enduring memory…"

Mark Henry Mepham is commemorated at Soissons Memorial, France, nearby to Louverval. Mark Henry was killed at Quenney Copse, at the retaking of the Somme battlefield, where Harry-Arthur had been fighting last.

Mark Mepham was killed on July 29, 1918, three months and eight days before the ceasefire, and armistice, November 1918. He was awarded the Victory Medal, posthumously.

As Walter, his body was not recovered.

Next pages: At the Hindenbourg Line, France, November 1917

Near Bourlon, 23 November 1917.

British troops going through a shattered village and forest, at the

plain of Cambrai ridge, 1917.

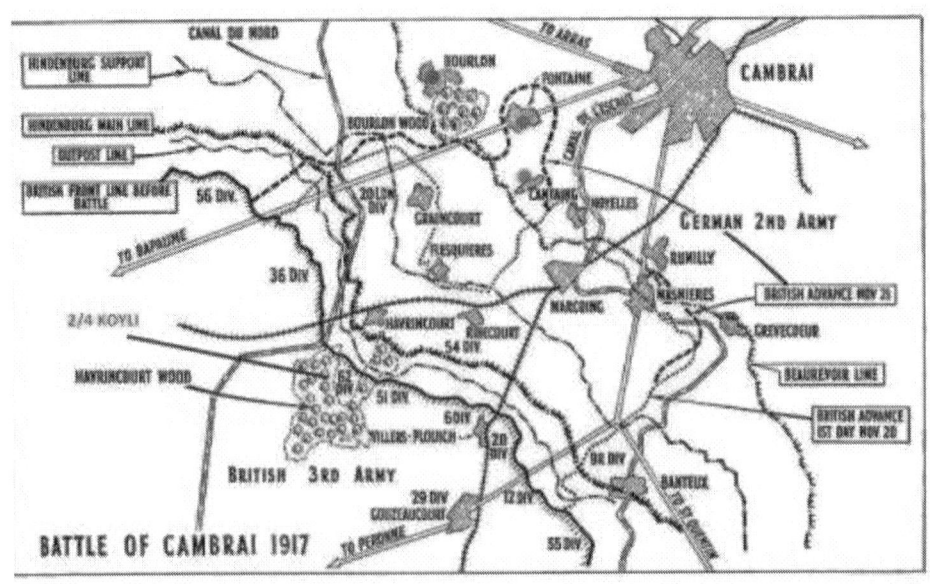

HINDENBURG SUPPORT LINE

HINDENBURG MAIN LINE
OUTPOST LINE

BRITISH FRONT LINE BEFORE
BATTLE

TO BAPAUME

CANAL DU NORD

TO ARRAS

BOURLON

FONTAINE

CAMBRAI

BOURLON WOOD

CANAL DE L'ESCAUT

56 DIV.

201TH
DIV

GRAINCOURT

CANTAING

NOYELLES

GERMAN 2ND ARMY

FLESQUIERES

36 DIV

RUMILLY

2/4 KOYLI

HAVRINCOURT

RIBECOURT

54 DIV

MARCOING

NESNIERES

BRITISH ADVANCE NOV 26

CREVECOEUR

HAVRINCOURT WOOD

62
DIV

51 DIV

60IV

VILLERS-PLOUICH

20
DIV

UR DIV

BANTEUX

BEAUREVOIR LINE

BRITISH ADVANCE
IST DAY NOV 20

BRITISH 3RD ARMY

29 DIV
GOUZEAUCOURT

12 DIV

TO PERONNE

55 DIV

BATTLE OF CAMBRAI 1917

Part Four: The Louverval Memorial, France. 14th March 1998.

Dear Walter,

I am back. I have been back. I have returned to this place many times. In just a few days, the cost of the battle of Cambrai amounted to fifty thousand German losses, and forty-five thousand Allied British and colonial lives. Altogether, a quarter of those taking part in the entire battle were lost.

For "the poor bloody infantry" the odds were not even; they were not even that good. In the newspapers, there was no mention aft the time or after of the "failed assault on Cambrai," as Conan Doyle latterly recorded, and took lofty notes for his war office reports; and hardly a word about the lowly infantry, except how many fell in numbers "as if as one great befalling."

Four miles of ground gained and lost again for nothing, except perhaps this: not victory that day, but the end of war, *that* war, had commenced. For all that, the bodies of the British and German and others fallen would provide nutrients for the ground then useless for growing anything. The gas and gunpowder rendered the soil dead for many years—decades—and it is only now slowly becoming fertile for growing flax and corn.

Of the people of Flesquieres, and all those other places passed through, who fled their villages, only some returned, and no one on either side or of any country returned home unscathed.

Men and women had been taken from their farms and dwellings and used as slave labour, digging the trenches of the Siegfried Line, and fighting bloody battles that only ended in victory, for all, on all sides, when that Great War ended.

Many had fallen, cannon fodder to the shells as we, unwittingly aided the death and demolition of the land that you, Walter, struggled across. God knows to where the women and children with their few possessions were gone.

Shrugging their shoulders. Gallic, Alsace, or Provençal, some returned, settled down with their children and children's children. The trees and woods had fallen, burnt alive, and all that was left were trampled muddy fields and concrete, and broken tanks.

Along the thousand-kilometre length of the Siegfried Line, the rivers flooded and canals and roads disappeared until there was nothing recognisable left for the people to return to.

But now, with new pastures seeded and life springing from the soil once again, you, my brother, Walter, you would not recognise it. A small cemetery field of white stone and a memorial arch has been erected amid pastoral grazed grasses again. The grains have been sown anew and harvested once more.

As our ancestors did with horse and plough, but now with great machines like the caterpillar tanks but great tractor-harvesters, cutting-down and threshing the wheat. The crops are now stored in great communal silos instead of each farm having its barn house, and the grain is ground to bread flour in great mechanical mills, for the bakers and their families to earn a living.

I did not cry much, Walter, when we learned of your being missing, and with certain lonely death. If only they could have brought you home. But they did not, and you did not come home. There were so many, so many who did not return...and you, my brother, a newspaper seller and short-lived bank post-room clerk, I a gamblers-den doorman in London.

But, you were among those who did not return at all; as was our father, Mark Henry. For us, and for our parents, the Great War was the ultimate gamble. When death was so close, living, fighting for life, day-by-day, hour by hour. We told ourselves we were fighting for us and our families, and our comrades at the front.

It was this that kept us going, somehow, and turned everything into a great adventure. An adventure the likes of which we could never have imagined, or wished to have imagined.

It was a chance to break out of our ordinary lives, and do something extraordinary, and seemingly greater than each of us alone. Except when it came to the actual death and dying—then it was easy to question things.

We were being sacrificed, but for what? To preserve the freedom of those dissenters and their families who stayed behind; or those who refused, or deserted?

As I did, too, eventually, as I did. As chance and fate would have it. Chance that I, Harry, was home that time. Fate that I was with Mother, and she knew not to let me return. Not for those Generals and Royalty and literary folk on the viewing posts, camped at the rear or tucked up in their beds back in England, or in prison.

We told ourselves, eventually, it was not for them. Not for our country, or for our Empire. No, once we were there, it was only for ourselves, our families, and for each other—comrades in arms, and at our paid work.

We *were* preserving our British and colonial way of life not at the risk of their being without accession, without succession, and possibly extinct without a personal existence beyond the grave; but ourselves.

When we heard about you, Walter, missing in action, I was on leave.

One of us had to survive, to carry on, as Mother said. I refused to go back. I ignored orders, deserted, and showed cowardice, perhaps, in the face of the enemy. What few understood, however, was that the enemy for me was not death itself. The enemy—for you, me, Mother, and Father—was the death of both of us.

Anyway, I gave myself up. I was arrested, and we knew I could face a firing squad. Hundreds deserted from the very start and more by the end—but as soon as we got to the front and found out what it was really like.

Early firing squad executions of such poor souls who fled the field, unable to face going on or going back. These assassinations were used, as I used you, as a warning to thousands who had not volunteered, or who had volunteered to something they could not possibly have imagined what no one could.

Like me, like us, they wanted to live; and could no longer kill, and by living, could let others live.

I was only reported for "absence without leave." I was arrested, detained, and sent back to Aldershot for incarceration. I can only wonder, now, how our father might have felt about it all. Mother knew all by then, and that I, at least, would survive.

Mother died in September of 1917, at Brighton, Sussex, aged fifty-two years.

Did Father know of Mother's dying, of whatever it was that killed her? Some disease from the front? Despair? Heartbreak? Knowing?

Perhaps Father knew about you, and then about Mother's death, somehow, *spiritually* perhaps, as Conan Doyle, our childhood hero, may have said.

We did not get any word back from Father. It was not customary to tell soldiers of deaths in their families while they were away, to keep up morale. And so, Father did not know about me deserting either, I am sure of that. He believed I was back at the

Western Front, and that we would meet up in our final victory.

With you and Mother, perhaps he knew, somehow, and it was already too much, and Father did not want to know the worst. His death, then, almost the more tragic: to be one of the last of those who would be killed, in the final months, days, hours, and minutes of war.

An end to hostilities was signed the eleventh minute of the eleventh hour of the eleventh day of November 1918, and June 30th 1919 The Entente between Britain and France was now truly Cordiale, with the German enemy the only remaining Central Power. The Tsar of Russia had already been assassinated along with his family; Russia would become enemies and allies again in the second World War in 1939 to 1945.

Believing that it had all come to an end, and that he had still a family to return to, Father took his part, as you had taken yours, in death.

I had taken mine in life, and for all of us, for life and family the same. I had taken mine, but differently. I had deserted duty to my King and Country, but not my Family. Father, Mark Henry Mepham, had finally been to North Africa. However, he would never actually see Morocco, that place of his dreams. He was one of the few survivors rescued at Gallipoli, Turkey, in 1915 with the Aussie and Anzac brigades. He was taken from there to Alexandria, Egypt, fighting the Germans and their allies across the deserts of North Africa to the end.

Then, in 1918, he was conveyed with the Fourth Battalion, from Alexandria, Egypt conflict, ended, to French Marseilles, to finish the job. With the remnants of the original British Expeditionary Force of 1914, he was moved up to Picardy, France, and Flanders, in June 1918.

In the final rout of the German armies, he was lost, killed in action at Quenney Copse, a small woodland, at the retaking of the Somme battlefield. Where I, Harry Arthur had not returned to, fro the third and final battle. Myself, I had fought there twice, and killed as well as escaped death.

Father was killed on 29 July 1918, the final days of the Somme, and victory; three months before the final armistice and ceasefire of the end of The Great War.

Father's body as yours, was not recovered. He was awarded the Victory Medal posthumously, at the Soissons memorial, France, near to where you, Walter, lie; and where you, Walter, brother, are remembered, here at Louverval, and always.

In November 1918, as a kind of reprieve for desertion while on leave, I was signed up again. This time to the twentieth regiment at the armistice, to hold the ground retaken in France and Flanders, and up to the Germany borders.

The would-be invaders were stopped, and we as good as invaded them instead.

The exhausted remains of the armies were returned home while we, along with the Americans and Canadians, with us in the west, and the soldiers of the new Communist Soviet Socialist Republic, of Russia, in the east.

The German armies retreated home. Finally pushed back and suing for peace at the Treaty of Versailles in 1919, the German democracy was returned. Hindenburg was to be tried as a war criminal, but he was never indicted. Kaiser Wilhelm abdicated in 1918, to the new German Republic, not to be replaced; and the King went into lifelong exile, to family in the still Monarchist Netherlands, and Belgium.

Tsar Nicholas was executed, shot dead with his family in 1918 following the Bolshevik communist revolution in Russia. King George remained on the throne of the Empire of Great Britain and Ireland.

Hindenburg was elected the first President of the Weimar Republic and at his death in August 1934, he surrendered the German Reichstag to Adolf Hitler, who, in 1914, had been a trench messenger, at the back trenches of Cambrai. A t the eventual allied victory there, the German Defeat in 1918.

Hitler bore that grudge fatally, as dictators often do, as Napoleon in 1815, again in 1945, at the end of the Second World War. Perhaps the Second World War was another case of unfinished business. In 1939, following the failure of British Prime Minister Chamberlain's pre-war appease-ment, Winston Churchill was again elected First Lord of the Admiralty, and this time for the duration of the Second World War with Nazi Germany, from 1939 to 1945.

Unfinished business.

The Second World War was a virtual repeat of the first. With the German invasion of Belgium and Northern France, again, and as with Russia, Britain stood alone in defence of our country and remains of our British Empire, at home and abroad.

Our enemy again this time, Germany bombed our homes and factories by air, in both directions destroying cities and lives again.

Until the Americans came in at the Normandy landings in France in 1944 and defeated Japan in the pacific with two nuclear bombs on Hiroshima and Nagasaki. The dictators Hitler and Hirohito were defeated in 1945, and democracy the victor since here at home, and in Europe and America, and most of the Empire, after mimicking dictatorships. China would become a new communist dictatorship under Mao Tse-Tung, as Russia was under Josef Stalin; and they would destroy many millions more lives, without the excuse of necessary war.

Nazi-Germany tried again to take over the British and French and Spanish and Portuguese Imperialist Empires and failed, again. As before, we all had victory, in eventual peace alone. War again failed, in the end; no winners, only survivors. Imperialists and dictators will always fail in the end, and their families fade away, as our family very nearly did, and as our British Empire continues to do, so; until it is no longer an empire but simply a monarchical-commonwealth of independent mostly democratic states, we and the world, all European, Global, and at Peace.

Sir Arthur Conan Doyle died at Windlesham Manor, Crowborough, Sussex, in 1930. After losing his eldest son, Kingsley, to injuries and pneumonia sustained at the Somme in 1918. He returned to agnostic spiritualism, and belief in a spiritual afterlife.

Of Bertrand Russell's two world wars of the twentieth century, Russell survived. It was a personal victory for both and their families, who might otherwise have all been slaughtered. As for all those who did fight, those who did not fight anymore; and all those, who lived again still a victory in the end for all, as for us.

As for us, Walter, Mother and Father, and as myself. Harry Arthur Mepham, Bertrand Russell had many children, and went on to start the Campaign for Nuclear Disarmament.

Although the League of Nations and the subsequent United Nations efforts have not ended war altogether, appeasement, peace talks, and decolonisation continues, oftentimes with their own war in India and Africa still.

There have been many more wars and partitioning of land, since 1945: India and Pakistan, then Bangla Desh, Sri Lanka. Korea, Vietnam, Cambodia. Ethiopia, Congo and Rwanda and Nigeria; Palestine and then Israel, and Egypt. Serbia, Kosovo, and Bosnia; Libya, and again in this 21st century, in Iran, Iraq, Afghanistan, and Syria.

With these wars comes disproportionate tribal and racial genocide every few years, this seems to happen a lot. Somewhere, most years: war and natural disasters, too.

Why? Because there is not enough food and homes to go around? There is, at least. If some had less; and more had more. Riches and greediness. Power and wealth. The Global Empires and their banks and Internet companies that is what it is all about now; as then, in 1914, World Trade.

Global Corporations, some of them larger than many small countries put together. Support, or are made to support, the largest countries with their former Empires. With five or six corporations in every sector, a few Global Corporations still now rule, where once

Monarchs and Dictators did. The religious, political, and personal racial and tribal vanities and hypocrisies of misguiding *leaders* persist, toward misguided individuals.

Brother and brother and sister and sister are set against each other. Wars of conquest, land, and natural resources to be taken from that land, including human populations.

One group over another, or attempting to be so. For trade, for the wealth of the planet. With the proliferation of nuclear weapons and after witnessing the horrors of two world wars, and the end the second at Hiroshima and Nagasaki, it is surely time for us to take to heart the later words of Winston Churchill: "…after all, when the mob rules, to jaw-jaw (or jaw to jaw) is always better than to war-war."

Maybe without the warmongering in 1914, we could have won a kind of brokered peace after all. The first time anyway, and maybe the Second World War would not have occurred, incurring such losses on all sides, and from all over the world.

But we will never know that.

Although we do know now that some attempt at appeasement was made by the Kaiser in 1914 and rejected, by his Generals, led by

President of the German Nation, General Bismarck. The German general, and dictators like Hitler, like Napoleon, may have then invaded England. The dictators may have taken command of the Baltic and the North German Sea now simply known everywhere as the North Sea.

But they did not.

And maybe only because we fought them when we did, and some, like you, Walter, and Father fought to the very end, and you and father gave with your precious lives.

The Central Powers and the Nazis may or may not have overrun our islands and our empire on which the sun has now been slowly setting. The British Commonwealth and European Union; North and South America; and Asia, China, and Australasian; and African trade groups are working to keep the peace in order to trade safely among each other. This seems merely a dream. But that is what we fought for, you and I, and after all that fighting, and refusing to fight anymore, it was not in vain.

I, Harry Arthur Mepham, was demobbed, "disembodied," it was called, and "dispersed" at Crystal Palace. I lived back in

Croydon, South London. I married in March 1922, another Gracie, and we survived through the post-war unemployment and economic Great Depression, which happened on both sides of the Atlantic, anyway.

Pensions were not paid to non-dependants, and those that were paid to surviving dependants were hardly worth anything, through devaluation of the currency. The old gold-standard for money, was gone. Churchill did that as Chancellor of the Exchequer between the wars, to attempt to fix the Great Depression predicted before the war was started. Maybe that *is* all we were fighting for? Gold, trade, and employment. Bread on the table; money in pocket.

There was a failed General Strike in 1926, but employment hours and conditions were eventually better controlled, and basic education became compulsory. Pensions came in for unemployment and old age; and only women over 30 years and with their own capital did get the right to vote in 1918; only later, before the next war, for the rest and full franchise as the men. And we held on to these victories after 1945, too.

Capitalism and Protectionist or Free-Trade borders in Europe, not fought over with weapons, but political and economic policies. I, became a newspaper printer and compositor at Gresham Street in London: 'Bread for our mouths and clothes on our backs…' as Father might have said. I am printing the news, rather than selling news, as you did, or making it, as we all did.

I…We. Had many children.

The first, Arthur Harry, was born in 1923 and fought in the Second World War in 1939. At twenty-one years, he was killed in France, in the Allied Normandy landings of D-day in 1944.

As our father, Mark Henry, was killed, shortly before the end of the Great War. So he, Harry Arthur, the second, as you Walter, gave up his life at the end of that World War.

Of ours, and every other family, all fought at home and abroad, and only some survived.

The Second World War was fought mostly from the air and sea this time, and on land using tanks and infantry; much as those at Cambrai; until the D-day landings in Europe, and the final rout again.

Some soldiers were conscripted in 1939 for National Service, and others volunteered. Many refused, had dependants, and worked in various protected trades and employment. Some went on the run and hid; and others signed-up, and then deserted. But we never heard about them. This news was too dangerous for the newspapers, or history, to tell. As *our* story, now is told.

So, did I encourage Our children to fight back in 1939? Or did I encourage you, as mother discouraged you, Walter, for that matter, myself, in 1917?

Knowing what could happen, what did happen?

No, and I did not encourage Arthur Harry to join up, but I let him make his own decision; I did not encourage you, Walter, and would not again, and it pains me yet, knowing what I know now, and what I knew then.

I would not have encouraged you, Walter, and did not so Arthur Harry, in 1939. For me to go in his place, as I would have, and you then died in my place. The conscription came in at the start of war that time 1939, for military training, war, and then afterwards National Service.

Many did refuse and despite everything that happened before, and knowing about you Walter, and seeing my eldest child for the last time, Arthur Harry went, and we had to let him go.

Arthur Harry, my son, your nephew, was killed like you, and father, in France, near the Somme. He knew about you, and Father.

The other of our children were younger, and they were evacuated, moved to safety outside of London. They went to stay with aunt Gracie (nee Wells) and her husband Walter Southgate, at their small holding in Ongar, Essex.

I stayed on in London with old Alf. Byfield, as a fire warden, Home Guard. Alf, who had refused the first time around, had children—daughters—born just after the First World War. Alf. and Etty's daughter Winifred Clara, married Albert Stow, at St Johns, Walthamstow, later in 1941.

With Alf. *that* second time around. Both of them, against the war, even though, or maybe despite, or maybe because his two elder brothers Harry and Archie did go, one in the Navy, one in the Army; and they survived. If Alf had gone to war that time before. The first time. Even as a non-combatant Pacifist. He would have stood as little chance as you and me in the fighting, and his children may not have been born. Nor their children's children, our cousins, second and third generations, and yet distant cousins to come.

Alf. Byfield, and Albert Stow of Walthamstow did their bit to keep the family and country alive, as I did; as we all did. When our father and me, went to war, back in 1914 they would not take him, being too old. So, he faked his age, and then I went, and then you Walter, came of age. I, Harry Arthur, your beloved brother, that second time I stayed behind.

I stayed with the Home Guard, like Conan Doyle before. To repel invasion, if it had happened. As in 1914 and then in 1940, as it was threatened again, afterwards, The Blitz on London, Cardiff, Coventry, Glasgow, Belfast. This country, England. These Great Islands of Great Britain and Ireland.

Partitioned following the successful Dublin Easter rising 1916, and provided safe air space, that bombed by air, torpedoed at sea, but no landed invasion, since the Normans, Germans, Italians and Spanish-Irish. Since 1066, and Viking Anglo-Saxon before that.

Air force battles were fought over England and sorties into France and Belgium to support second wave of landing craft at Dunkirk. Instead, an heroic retreat from Dunkirk, to the heroic D-Day landings along Normandy coast.

As that first time around the Nazi's bombed London, and perhaps did want to take back the islands that the Anglo-Saxons had peopled. From the ancient Britons, Celts and Vikings, Romans and Normans. Irish and Welsh and Scots and English ancient early Great Britons.

All those centuries back then. Germans, Franks, Latin Mediterraneans, African, and Asian, and from all corners of the once Empire; and who did fight with us.

They, as we, reside here, on our islands now; and we mix and change as they did, we do.

If I had gone back, Walter, after you were lost, and been killed as well; then they, your nieces and nephews, would not be here. They would not have been born.

After the First World War, through the 1920s, I watched our children grow up and become parents, and we became grandparents. I watched over our children, your nieces and nephews, and now our grandchildren are growing-up, and marrying into other families.

So, we Mephams and Wells, we go on.

Everyone in the family was mostly named after each other. No one else was named Walter after you. Walter Southgate, who lived to a ripe old age, and was presented to a Socialist Labour Party, conference as one of the originating members.

It might have been bad luck, afterward, to take your name, Walter. Anyway, it would not have been right not to be done, not after what happened.

There are many Harrys though; and another Mark and Caroline, and with them; another Harry-Arthur now in Sussex, at the close of this 20th century. European Union of this 21st Century.

Now that the Great War is done, and that second Great War too, another Harry is born at Hastings, Sussex. So, together now, we have our children: cousins, nieces, nephews, and their children, too. So many of them. We have our father and mother, and now our story is told. Our grandparents, and their parents before them, and you, my brother, Walter. Now your story too is told; and mine, and the both of ours now, to carry on…

Your loving brother, Harry Arthur Mepham 1895-

Postscript. Louverval 30th November 2017.

The voluntary military covenant in the United Kingdom is enshrined as the Ministry of Defence view that "serving soldiers should expect to be valued and respected as individuals, and that they and their families are sustained, and rewarded." A serving British soldier, who is a last surviving sibling, is given permanent home leave if requested.

In 1948, the sole survivor policy in the US military was introduced for brothers not to be attached to the same unit and to be excluded from the draft in wartime, so that one brother at least has a better chance of remaining to continue the family line. Although voluntary, these policies have been enshrined in real and cinematic life (*Saving Private Ryan*, 1998). This also applies, in most cases, to sisters who fight on the front lines.

In 2002, Britain and the United States, along with various allied forces, went to war in Iraq based on the lie of weapons of mass destruction, later shown to be false propaganda for the purpose, it then seemed, of waging another Great War: a War on Terror.

Despite the rocket-launchers and strategic ballistic ground-to-air missiles. As well as drones and suicide bombers, to attempt to terrify populations, we are only made stronger.

Warfare, today, like some kind of Great Third World War. Is not as before; and we should never make those mistakes again. It is a war of Middle Eastern Semitic cousins and brothers, of the Zionist and Islamist states and secular conscripting males, and females, and children from every family. Fighting globally to retain or capture land, and what land has not been captured and settled at some time in history? Now, with nuclear power, with Arabian and African, and Russian oil and gas.

Another 'World War', except we say Global War now.

A War of and on Terror, worldwide. Stopped and started again somewhere else. As if the previous World Wars of the twentieth century had not been started…but then we could go all the way back through history…as of 2014 Russia invaded Crimea, as they did in 1865, and that famous poem was written. As The Russian Federation has replaced the Soviet Union after the fall of the Berlin Wall and the Cold War, ancient Colonial borders are still being fought over in Asia and Africa and all for Trade and Drug Wars, fought all over the world, challenging trade, and peace.

Re-populated borders are re-written in the aftermath of wars, and as perhaps borders will continue, they will always to be fought over. Old empires re-emerge and are revised.

The War on Terror is not a war on terror. It is a war *of* terror.

It could better be referred to as The Fuel Wars, for cheap gas and oil; or The Money Wars, or Cyber-Wars. Or simply be called The Weapon's Wars. Virtual, or real.

After the collapse of the Berlin Wall, and near-collapse of global world banking, at the start of this new century, another depression dip occurred in the economy, and became a global crisis. We are told. Despite religious and other unconscionable excuses otherwise, these same Trade Wars are fought as viciously and desperately as any war since the dawn of civilisation.

Following the bombing of the World Trade Center in New York on 11 September 2001, invasions of Afghanistan, Iraq, and now Syria by the west and east, and the so-called Arab Uprisings, Money Credit-Boom and Banking-Crash.

Wars in Libya, West and East Africa. Wars as battles, in Georgia and Chechnya, and Ukraine and Crimea, again. The Russian Federation; and now Turkey, Syria, and Iraq again, from Saudi to

Sudan and Yemen, the same great swathes of ex-Colonial Central Africa.

From Somalia to Nigeria, as well as the Israeli-Palestine battle, continues, endlessly it seems. But then so did apartheid in South Africa seem forever, but for peace and reconciliation.

Now, The World is like a Third World War computer-game, but for real.

With soldiers entrenched behind digital screens and computer-screens, with remotely controlled roadside-bombs and armoured-vehicles, and rocket-launchers, on land, in the skies nuclear-armed planes, 'artificial' intelligence, and battle-drones.

Yet, everything still is money, power, and trade, the same as before, and each of us can only eat and consume so much. Policies like the Strategic Arms Limitation Talks and treaties, continuing to reduce weaponry and hostilities amongst buffer zones; newly independent states with democratic non-monopoly trading relationships, may be the only way now. In the early second decade of this twenty-first century.

We may attempt to limit the escalation of conflict, through peaceful trade agreements, and continuous peace and reconciliation.

Rather than a re-doing of the most atrocious acts globally, rape and torture, starvation.

We as a people learn from our history, for ourselves and other's lessons, and stop repeating the same mistakes? Armies of Humanitarian Aid! Not armies of pirates and privateers. Yet the aid is too often squandered and stolen, by the new dictators, and there are plenty of them. This is and may continue to be, the more usual international response to such outrageous wars, of theft and revenge, and body bags arriving home. The slaughtering of thousands, or even a few, or one.

Outrage and atrocities to deliberately Shock and Awe, and reap converts to the cause religious or political. To begin and continue unwinnable wars, using invasion and insurgency from all sides; now from the air and possibly Outer-Space in this Twenty-First Century.

The Cold War between capitalist America and communist Russia ended in the last century, with the fall of the Berlin Wall.

Global-Trade deals continue in the relative peace of a kind of perpetual battle, which may never disappear. Like the computer games we now play: like The Stock-Markets.

The Banks and the Social Media we follow and blog and blag about: The Global Religious and Fuel-Money-Cyber Trade-Wars, as we may now call the tendency toward Total World Domination.

Are perpetuated by a final hopeless few, who only really believe in permanent perpetual war, without end.

What other end is there? Suicide missions and bombings and executions are still with us. Still daily somewhere on the globe. Maybe men and women will always go to war, to protect and defend their own family and others' families, as we see it, for ourselves; at the time bread for the table, money for the pocket.

For Global-Trade? For survival? For impossible ends? For (relative) Peace? Everywhere?

Maybe we will not always so readily deny responsibility for each other, and each other's families, for all of us are family.

Our decision to go to war starts at home, and at the time no-doubt called-for and fought for our own selfish and self-righteous ends, perhaps. In the end, war can only ever be for reconciliation and peace. So why even start a war?

Through the ability to truthfully discuss and resolve problems, issues, when no-one is starving, or seeking shelter, there is no need for war.

Perhaps we, the human species, will never learn the lessons of the past, perhaps always fight and make peace, perhaps learn something new, but always fight again and again.

Each of us fights every day, battles at least. For family, for livelihoods, and whatever else is on radio and television, social-networking, worth fighting for, standing-up at least.

Trolling if we are not careful with what we say and do, starting another war. Cyber-War. Virtual war, as they could then, back in 1917, imagine only in the science fiction of the Conan Doyle stories; or be warned of by the pacifist peace-makers as Bertrand Russell.

Perhaps we all will learn to live peacefully together, without starting wars, over a single outrage, assassination, like in Sarajevo, committed video'd and social-media'd?

All of us *spiritually*, not only us ourselves and our families, but with all others, too.

Maybe there is a real democratic ratio of for and against war at any stage? Perhaps a vociferous, then popular assumed majority that starts wars; in the end another quiet majority, that finishes, or refuses to start wars in the first place, despite the regular battles of life, no one gets killed.

Sports and Games can both provide and take away. At some point, people refuse to go on in hatred and fear, refuse to fight any longer. Live to provide for ourselves and others.

Or talk and play along, ignoring the reality of wanton death and destruction, or feeling unable to do anything about it.

If we can, we, most of us, spend all of our time avoiding war, avoiding conflict, that is. Walking down the street, meeting at work, at home; and we generally take few chances, generally avoiding conflict at all costs.

Defusing the words, bombs, and bullets of fear and hatred, we can act in favour and blessing, with family, friends, and strangers, stepping out of the way, turning away from the given scene, literally we would hope, to take ourselves and family, friends and strangers, to relative safety.

We do this seeking of peace and reconciliation, everyday of our lives. All the time. From lies and ignorance in personal deception and denial of our own actions, of our willingness to fight, or not. Owning our actions and decisions with integrity whatever they are, and listening to others.

Living, listening to what others think and to believe. In self, and family, and society, and people, and everywhere, the world appreciating actions and words, as well as our own.

To feed and protect ourselves and our families, as we see it at the time maybe threatened, by a sense of in-justice, and dis-enfranchised. But by coming to acceptable terms, we can speak out for safety and security.

Most of us all the time for faith and no faith, except in each other, secular, and political neither psychologically, physically, nor cynically violent, but generally non-violent, at any moment in time. We always seek peace in the end, always, even in war! So why go to war in the first place?

Ourselves within our family, and those with whom we are in daily contact, are our priority not to kill or be killed.

Perhaps one day there will be no more wars. No more battles that cannot be sorted out democratically gradually, not instantaneously, but with persistent kind words and kind deeds.

Until then, in any wartime already started, once the decision is made, it is made integrally and sincerely for then. And for ourselves, as others, forever, it now seems, eternally. Although wars may be started, from: unthinking and deliberate anger and hatred. Real fear, and a perceived excuse of necessity.

Eventually, in peace and reconciliation as any decision in life, that we should not be expected to take of ourselves or another, either to kill, or be killed; or not have any family killed, at home, or abroad.

For all peoples. To war permanently for anyone or for all peoples is impossible anyway, without ourselves and those we love, all being killed in the process. To live in perfect peace and love for always, may seem humanly, naturally impossible, but always we must keep trying.

In righteousness and wrongfulness, in redemption, and with honest understanding once committed, any act of history can only ever be assuaged, by an honest, accurate and truthful personal account, peace, and redemption,

For yours and for my family, now, too,

Harry Arthur Walter Mepham born 1998, Hastings, Sussex, England. This Remembrance, Armistice Day, Louverval, France 2017. Aged nineteen years. Love and Peace.

The eleventh hour of the eleventh day of the eleventh month 2018.

Notes

All quotations, except where otherwise indicated, are from Conan Doyle's *The British Campaign in France and Flanders*, published in 1928 in six volumes.

Bertrand Russell's "The Ethics of War" was printed in the *International Journal of Ethics*, January 1915, and discussed in the newspapers of the time until suppressed to the end of the Great War (1914–18).

Winston Churchill (1874-1965) quote from a speech at the White House, Washington D.C. June 26th 1954 with President Eisenhower following United Nations Day June 24th.

All photographs acknowledged and copied with permissions sought.

Chronology of events:
1798 French Revolution and Napoleonic Empire and War.
1805 Great grandfather William Mepham born, Kent.
1812 Napoleon retreats from Moscow.
1815 Battle of Waterloo. Napoleon defeated by Wellington and Blucher's armies.

1831 Grandfather Mark born, Kent.
1831 Great grandmother Harriet dies, Sussex.

1851 Mark Mepham marries Fanny (Henry?) of Sussex.
1851 Great Grandfather William dies.
1851 aunt Francis Lucy born at Bishopstone, Sussex.
1852 Father Mark Henry born Bishopstone, Sussex.

1852 Conan Doyle born Edinburgh.

1856 Flood at The Tide Mills.

1865 mother Caroline Wells born Old Ford, Middlesex (east).

1865 Crimean War, Russia.
1869 Suez Canal opened.
1871 Peace Treaty at Versailles, France. Prussian War ended and German Monarchy restored ruled by Generals under Bismark.
1880-1 and 1889-1902 German-Dutch Boer wars, south Africa.

1891 Mark Mepham and Caroline Wells married.

1892 Bertrand Russell born Wales.

1895 Harry Arthur born Hampshire.

1898 Walter Mepham born Paddington London.

1898 Grandmother Harriet dies in Hampshire and buried in Sussex.

1906 Conan Doyle moves from Edinburgh to Windlesham Manor, Crowhurst, Sussex.
1907 Entente Cordiale between Britain and France, and Russia, and Belgium.

1908 Cousin Etty (nee Wells) marries Alf. Byfield. Family moves to Walthamstow, Essex.
1908 Uncle Arthur marries Clara Wilson.

1910 Mark Henry and Caroline Mepham family move to Stedham Chambers, Holborn, London.

1914-18 World War One.
1916 The Easter revolutionary uprising Dublin.
1917 The Russian Soviet Communist revolution.
1917 Walter Mepham killed at Cambrai.

1921 Harry Arthur marries Grace, first child Arthur Harry.

1939-1945 second World War. Arthur Harry killed in France. Nuclear bomb dropped on Hiroshima and Nagasaki.

1930 Conan Doyle dies at Crowborough.

1957 Russell and many others start the Campaign for Nuclear Disarmament (CND) in London, and worldwide.

1970 Bertrand Russell dies. Wales.

1998 Harry Arthur Walter Mepham, born, Hastings, Sussex.
2000 Harry Arthur Mepham dies, Sussex, England.
2001 ?

V186562

Walter Mepham
Born March 14 1898
Killed November 30 1917
Cambrai France

POST · CARD

Also by M. Stow

EarthCentre: The End of the Universe

Universal Verses

Pan Tan-Gou: Paradise Won!

ArcTol

WarFair4

28639979R00107

Made in the USA
Columbia, SC
14 October 2018